# *Pleasu*

Here is a collection of stories, jokes, riddles, tongue-twisters, poems, limericks, incredible facts, things to do and even magic tricks – something for every occasion and every mood. It is a real treasure chest to rummage in when you are bored, or it's wet, or you want to amuse your friends or yourself. The book is roughly divided into people, food, growing things, time and seasons, birds and beasts, magic and marvels and fun with words; some things are funny and some are serious but all are entertaining in the widest sense. The book will be especially enjoyed by people of nine and over.

# Pleasure Trove

Jennifer Curry

*Illustrated by William Geldart*

Beaver Books

Published by
The Hamlyn Publishing Group Limited
London · New York · Sydney · Toronto
Astronaut House, Feltham, Middlesex, England


ISBN 0 600 37127 1

Printed in England by
Cox and Wyman Limited
London, Reading and Fakenham
Set in Monotype Garamond
Diagrams by Robin Anderson

# *Acknowledgements*

The author and publishers would like to thank the following people for giving permission to include in this anthology material which is their copyright:

William Blackwood and Sons Limited for 'Daddy Fell into the Pond' from *Daddy Fell into the Pond and other Poems* by Alfred Noyes

The Bodley Head for the extract from *Beowulf: Dragon Slayer* by Rosemary Sutcliff

Jonathan Cape Limited for 'I Like That Stuff' from *Poems* by Adrian Mitchell

Coronet Books for 'Social Mechanism' from *Grooks* by Piet Hein

The Author's Literary Estate and Chatto and Windus Limited for 'Extremely Naughty Children' from *Green Outside* by Elizabeth Godley

Mrs William Croft Dickinson and Susan Gibson for the extract from *Borrobil* by William Croft Dickinson

Dennis Dobson Publishers for 'Good Company' from *Good Company* by Leonard Clark

J. M. Dent and Sons Limited and The Trustees for the Copyrights of the late Dylan Thomas for the extract from *Under Milk Wood* by Dylan Thomas

Gerald Durrell and Rupert Hart-Davis for the extract from *My Family and Other Animals* by Gerald Durrell

Edinburgh University Press for 'The Computer's First Christmas Card' by Edwin Morgan

Faber and Faber Limited for 'My Aunt' from *Meet my Folks* by Ted Hughes; the extract from *The Country Child* by Alison Uttley; and 'The Naming of Cats' from *Old Possum's Book of Practical Cats* by T. S. Eliot

Faber and Faber Limited and Doubleday and Company Incorporated for 'The Serpent' from *Collected Poems* by Theodore Roethke

Collection Haags Gemeentemuseum – The Hague for the woodcut 'Sky and Water 1' from *The Graphic Work of M. C. Escher*

William Heinemann Limited for 'Mr Tom Narrow' from *The Wandering Moon* by James Reeves; and 'Making Stew' from *Delight* by J. B. Priestley

Michael Joseph Limited and M. and J. Hobbs for 'The Pig' from *Milligan's Ark* by Edward Lucie-Smith

Mr Arthur S. Pederson and Doubleday and Company Incorporated for 'The Flower-cart Man' from *Taxis and Toadstools* by Rachel Field

Punch Publications Limited for 'Wanted' by Daniel Pettiward

Ian Serraillier for 'Piano Practice' (© Copyright Ian Serraillier 1963)

Sidgwick and Jackson Limited for 'Moonlit Apples' from *Collected Poems* by John Drinkwater; and 'Ducks' by F. W. Harvey

Mrs James Thurber for the extract from *The Wonderful O* by James Thurber (© Copyright 1957 James Thurber. Published by Simon and Schuster, New York)

Mrs Ann Thwaite for *The Kangaroo's Coff* by Anthony Thwaite

Mrs Iris Wise, Macmillan, London and Basingstoke, and The Macmillan Company of Canada for 'Little Things' from *Collected Poems* by James Stephens

## *Introduction*

*Pleasure Trove* doesn't need any introduction from me – Adrian Mitchell has said it all in the first poem. It's simply a collection of 'stuff that I like'. I hope you like it too.

*Jennifer Curry* 1976

# *I Like That Stuff*

Lovers lie around in it
Broken glass is found in it
Grass
I like that stuff

Tuna fish get trapped in it
Legs come wrapped in it
Nylon
I like that stuff

Eskimos and tramps chew it
Madame Tussaud gave status to it
Wax
I like that stuff

Elephants get sprayed with it
Scotch is made with it
Water
I like that stuff

Clergy are dumbfounded by it
Bones are surrounded by it
Flesh
I like that stuff

Harps are strung with it
Mattresses are sprung with it
Wire
I like that stuff

Carpenters make cots of it
Undertakers use lots of it
Wood
I like that stuff

Cigarettes are lit by it
Pensioners are happy when they sit by it
Fire
I like that stuff

Dankworth's alto is made of it, most of it,
Scoobdedoo is composed of it
Plastic
I like that stuff

Man made fibres and raw materials
Old rolled gold and breakfast cereals
Platinum linoleum
I like that stuff

Skin on my hands
Hair on my head
Toenails on my feet
And linen on my bed

Well I like that stuff
Yes I like that stuff
The earth
Is made of earth
And I like that stuff

*Adrian Mitchell*

# *Extremely Naughty Children*

By far
The naughtiest
Children
I know
Are Jasper
Geranium
James
And Jo.

They live
In a house
On the Hill
Of Kidd,
And what
In the world
Do you think
They did?

They asked
Their Uncles
And Aunts
To tea,
And shouted
In loud,
Rude voices
'We

Are tired
Of scoldings
And sendings
To bed;
Now
The grown-ups
Shall be
Punished instead.'

They said:
'Auntie Em,
You didn't
Say 'Thank you!'
They said:
'Uncle Robert,
We're going
To spank you!'

They pulled
The beard
Of Sir Henry
Dorner
And put him
To stand
In disgrace
In the corner.

They scolded
Aunt B.
They punished
Aunt Jane;
They slapped
Aunt Louisa
Again
And again.

They said
'Naughty boy!'
To their
Uncle
Fred,
And boxed
His ears
And sent him
To bed.

Do you think
Aunts Em
And Loo
And B.,
And Sir
Henry
Dorner
(K.C.B.)

And the elderly
Uncles
And kind
Aunt Jane
Will go
To tea
With the children
Again?

*Elizabeth Godley*

## BRAIN BOTHERER

Pointing to one of the family portraits in the banqueting hall, the earl remarked, 'Brother and sister have I none, but that man's father is my father's son.' How was he related to the man in the picture?

## *Brown's Baby*

Brown has a lovely baby girl,
The stork left her with a flutter;
Brown, he named her 'Margarine',
For he hadn't any but her.

# RIDICULOUS RIDDLES

Q. What do you call a man who inspects rabbit holes?

A. A borough surveyor.

Q. What is yellow and jumps from cake to cake?

A. Tarzipan.

Q. What is the difference between a lazy schoolboy and a fisherman?

A. One hates his books – the other baits his hooks.

# TONGUE TWISTER

My wife swiped Mr Snipe's wife's knife.

# *Daddy Fell into the Pond*

Everyone grumbled. The sky was gray.
We had nothing to do and nothing to say.
We were nearing the end of a dismal day,
And there seemed to be nothing beyond,
THEN
Daddy fell into the pond!

And everyone's face grew merry and bright,
And Timothy danced for sheer delight.
'Give me the camera, quick, oh quick!
He's crawling out of the duckweed.' Click!

Then the gardener suddenly slapped his knee,
And doubled up, shaking silently,
And the ducks all quacked as if they were daft
And it sounded as if the old drake laughed.

Oh, there wasn't a thing that didn't respond
WHEN
Daddy fell into the pond!

*Alfred Noyes*

## *Piano Practice*

A doting father once there was
Who loved his daughter Gerda,
Until she got the piano craze –
Then how the passion stirred her!
Her fingers were wild elephants' feet,
And as month after month he heard her
He tried every way
To stop her play
From bribery to murder.

One day when she was practising,
He popped up behind and caught her
And dumped her in his wheelbarrow
And carried her off to slaughter.
Tipping her into a well, he cried,
'Hurrah! I've drowned my daughter!'
But a voice from the well
Rang out like a bell,
'Aha – there isn't any water!'

*Ian Serraillier*

# *Mr Tom Narrow*

A scandalous man
Was Mr Tom Narrow,
He pushed his grandmother
Round in a barrow.
And he called out loud
As he rang his bell,
'Grannies to sell!
Old grannies to sell!'

The neighbours said,
As he passed them by,
'This poor old lady
We will not buy.
He surely must be
A mischievous man
To try for to sell
His own dear Gran!'

'Besides,' said another,
'If you ask me,
She'd be very small use
That I can see.'
'You're right,' said a third,
'And no mistake –
A very poor bargain
She'd surely make.'

So Mr Tom Narrow,
He scratched his head,
And he sent his grandmother
Back to bed;
And he rang his bell
Through all the town
Till he sold his barrow
For half-a-crown.

*James Reeves*

## *Scottish Children's Song*

Oh ye cannae shove yer grannie off the bus,
No, ye cannae shove yer grannie off the bus,
Oh ye cannae shove yer grannie
For she's yer mammie's mammie –
Ye cannae shove yer grannie off the bus.

## FASCINATING FACT

Did you know that:

Anne Boleyn, the second wife of Henry VIII, wore gloves all the time to hide the fact that she had six fingers on her left hand?

# Kings and Queens

'I know I have the body of a weak and feeble woman, but I have the heart and stomach of a king, and of a king of England too.'

*Elizabeth I of England on the approach of the Spanish Armada*

'I want there to be no peasant in my kingdom so poor that he cannot have a chicken in his pot every Sunday.'

*Henri IV of France*

'I am the Martyr of the People.'

*Charles I of England, in his speech from the scaffold*

'If I were not king, I should lose my temper.'

*Louis XIV of France*

'I will be good.'

*Victoria, on becoming Queen of England*

'I'm really quite an ordinary sort of chap.'

*George V of England, at his Jubilee*

## FAMOUS FALLACY

Did you know that:

Queen Marie-Antoinette did *not* say 'Let them eat cake' when she heard that her people had no bread to eat.

# Miss Havisham

In an arm-chair, with an elbow resting on the table and her head leaning on that hand, sat the strangest lady I have ever seen, or shall ever see.

She was dressed in rich materials – satins, and lace, and silks – all of white. Her shoes were white. And she had a long white veil dependent from her hair, and she had bridal flowers in her hair, but her hair was white. Some bright jewels sparkled on her neck and on her hands, and some other jewels lay sparkling on the table. Dresses, less splendid than the dress she wore, and half-packed trunks, were scattered about. She had not quite finished dressing, for she had but one shoe on – the other was on the table near her hand – her veil was but half arranged, her watch and chain were not put on, and some lace for her bosom lay with those trinkets, and with her handkerchief, and gloves, and some flowers, and a Prayer-Book, all confusedly heaped about the looking-glass.

It was not in the first moments that I saw all these things, though I saw more of them in the first moments than might be supposed. But I saw that everything within my view which ought to be white, had been white long ago, and had lost its lustre, and was faded and yellow. I saw that the bride within the bridal dress had withered like the dress, and like the flowers, and had no brightness left but the brightness of her sunken eyes. I saw that the dress had been put upon the rounded figure of a young woman, and that the figure upon which it now hung loose, had shrunk to skin and bone. Once, I had been taken to one of our old marsh churches to see a skeleton in the ashes of a rich dress, that had been dug out of a vault under the church pavement. Now the skeleton seemed to have dark eyes that moved and looked at me. I should have cried out, if I could.

*from* Great Expectations *by Charles Dickens*

Which of the people in the picture is the tallest? When you have decided, find a ruler and measure them all, and find out if you were right.

## *Starting a Game*

One-ery, two-ery, ziccary, zan;
Hollow bone, crackabone, ninery ten:
Spittery spot, it must be done;
Twiddledum, twaddledum, twenty-one.
Hink spink, the puddings stink,
The fat begins to fry,
Nobody's at home, but jumping Joan,
Father, mother and I.
Stick, stock, stone dead,
Blind men can't see,
Every knave will have a slave,
You or I must be HE.

Mena, deena, deina, duss,
Catala, weena, weina, wuss,
Spit, spot, must be done,
Twiddlum, twaddlum, twenty-one!
OUT spells out and out you must go.

## *Ball-bouncing Game*

Long-legged Italy
Kicked poor Sicily
Into the middle of the Mediterranean Sea.
Austria was Hungary,
Took a bit of Turkey,
Dipped it in Greece,
Fried it in Japan,
And ate it off China.

## *Skipping Song*

The High Skip,
The Sly Skip,
The Skip like a Feather,
The Long Skip,
The Strong Skip,
And the Skip All Together.

The Slow Skip,
The Toe Skip,
The Skip Double-Double,
The Fast Skip,
The Last Skip,
And the Skip Against Trouble.

## *Conkers*

Iddy, iddy, onker,
My first conker,
Iddy, iddy, oh,
My first go.

The bottle of perfume that Willie sent
Was highly displeasing to Millicent;
Her thanks were so cold,
They quarrelled, I'm told,
Through that silly scent Willy sent Millicent.

There was a young fellow called Fisher
Who was fishing for fish in a fissure.
Then a cod with a grin
Pulled the fisherman in . . .
Now they're fishing the fissure for Fisher.

There was an old man from Nantucket
Who kept all his cash in a bucket.
His daughter, named Nan,
Ran away with a man,
And as for the bucket, Nan took it.

# Something to Do – Pipe-cleaner People

You will need five pipe-cleaners for each figure, some tissue paper, coloured paper, wool, thread, glue and scraps of material.

To begin, take one pipe-cleaner and leave 3 cm at the top end to form the neck. Make your second and third cleaners into arms by forming a small loop at one end of each of them for hands, making a bend where the shoulders should be, and then twisting the rest of each around the body part of the first cleaner, from the neck downwards.

Do the same with the two legs, making a loop at one end of each for the foot, bending each at the knee, and twisting the rest neatly around the body.

A little ball of tissue paper can be made into a head, tied tightly at the neck with thread. Cut circles of coloured paper as the eyes and mouth, make the hair from strands of wool, and glue these into place.

You can dress these figures, if you wish, with skirts, trousers and tops made from scraps of material, and then they can be hung up by threads as mobiles, pinned upright to a board with a drawing pin through each foot, or bent into interesting positions like clowns or gymnasts.

## *It Couldn't Be Done*

Somebody said that it couldn't be done,
But he, with a grin, replied
He'd never be one to say it couldn't be done –
Leastways, not till he'd tried.
So he buckled right in, with a trace of a grin,
By golly, he went right to it.
He tackled The Thing That Couldn't Be Done!
And he couldn't do it.

# BRAIN BOTHERER

Two Abyssinians enter a hotel and, as they are signing the visitors' book, explain to the proprietor that one of them is the father of the other Abyssinian's son. How are they related to each other?

## *Grace for a Child*

Here a little child I stand,
Heaving up my either hand;
Cold as paddocks though they be,
Here I lift them up to Thee,
For a benison to fall
On our meat, and on us all.

*Robert Herrick*

## *Playground Song*

The sausage is a cunning bird
With feathers long and wavy;
It swims about the frying pan
And makes its nest in gravy.

## *from* Delight

Making stew. It is not often I am allowed to do this; and indeed my great stew-making time was during the darker hours of the war, when anything was about to happen. But I am always delighted to make stew. And it is unusually good stew. You might travel from Truro to Inverness, even today, and be offered nothing better than or as good as my stew. One of my children, without any prompting from me, once ate four large helpings of it. My stew is thick, nourishing and wonderfully tasty. It has meat in it, but almost any kind of meat will do. I add all vegetables that are in season and in the house. And when I am in the mood I toss in exquisite little dumplings. After hours of simmering and thickening and thinning, for I never rush the business and keep peering into the pan, tasting, muttering a spell or two, I add any red wine that I can lay my hands on, and then, at the last moment, drop in a spoonful of honey. The stew is then ready. The very smell is princely. All men and all children gobble my stew gratefully. The women, who hate us to master their little arts, pretend to taste dubiously, arch their brows, wrinkle their noses, ask what is in it, complain about the mess in the kitchen; but nevertheless they contrive in a rather absent-minded manner to eat their share of the noble dish. How can they help it? Here is a stew that has been seasoned with many onions, red wine and honey – and my delight.

*J. B. Priestley*

An epicure, dining at Crewe,
Found quite a large mouse in his stew.
Said the waiter, 'Don't shout,
Or wave it about,
Or the rest will be wanting one too!'

There was once a young lady of Ryde
Who ate a green apple and died;
The apple fermented
Inside the lamented,
And made cider inside her inside.

It was just as I knew it would be,
I sat next to the Duchess at tea.
The noises abdominal
Were something phenomenal –
And everyone thought it was ME!

# *from* Alice through the Looking Glass

Alice glanced nervously along the table, as she walked up the large hall, and noticed that there were about fifty guests, of all kinds: some were animals, some birds, and there were even a few flowers among them. 'I'm glad they've come without waiting to be asked,' she thought: 'I should never have known who were the right people to invite!'

There were three chairs at the head of the table: the Red and White Queens had taken two of them, but the middle one was empty. Alice sat down, rather uncomfortable at the silence, and longing for some one to speak.

At last the Red Queen began. 'You've missed the soup and fish,' she said. 'Put on the joint!' And the waiters set a leg of mutton before Alice, who looked at it rather anxiously, as she had never had to carve one before.

'You look a little shy: let me introduce you to that leg of mutton,' said the Red Queen. 'Alice – Mutton: Mutton – Alice.' The leg of mutton got up in the dish and made a little bow to Alice; and she returned the bow, not knowing whether to be frightened or amused.

'May I give you a slice?' she said, taking up the knife and fork, and looking from one Queen to the other.

'Certainly not,' the Red Queen said, very decidedly: 'it isn't etiquette to cut any one you've been introduced to. Remove the joint!' And the waiters carried it off, and brought a large plum-pudding in its place.

'I won't be introduced to the pudding, please,' Alice said rather hastily, 'or we shall get no dinner at all. May I give you some?'

But the Red Queen looked sulky, and growled 'Pudding – Alice: Alice – Pudding. Remove the pudding!' and the waiters took it away before Alice could return its bow.

However, she didn't see why the Red Queen should be the only one to give orders, so, as an experiment, she called out 'Waiter! Bring back the pudding!' and there it was again in a moment, like a conjuring trick. It was so large that she couldn't help feeling a *little* shy with it, as she had been with the mutton: however, she conquered her shyness by a great

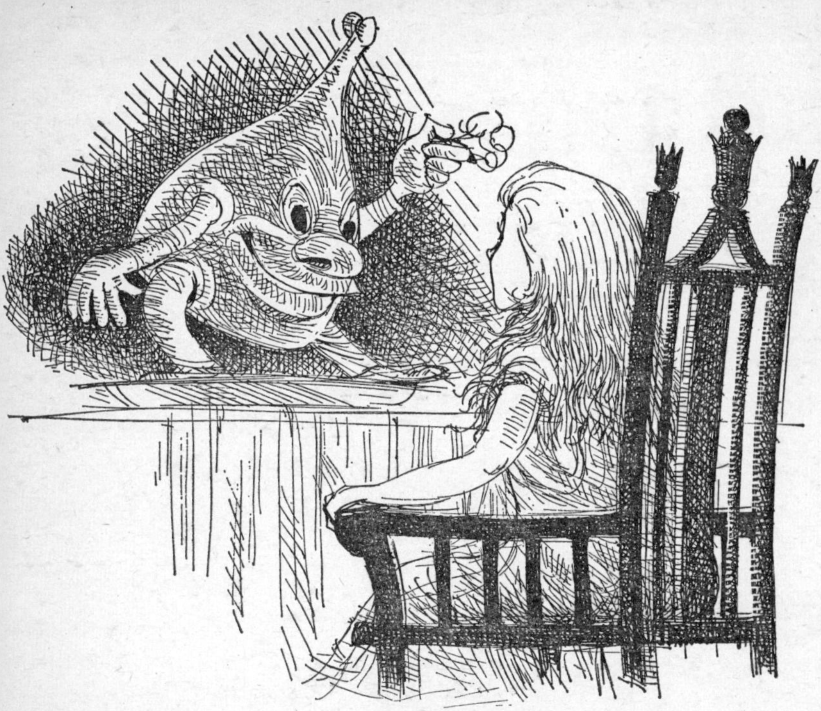

effort, and handed a slice to the Red Queen.

'What impertinence!' said the Pudding. 'I wonder how you'd like it, if I were to cut a slice out of *you*, you creature!'

It spoke in a thick, suety sort of voice, and Alice hadn't a word to say in reply: she could only sit and look at it and gasp.

'Make a remark,' said the Red Queen: 'it's ridiculous to leave all the conversation to the pudding!'

*Lewis Carroll*

T–PT–B

# RIDICULOUS RIDDLES

Q. Why did the jam-roll?

A. Because it saw the apple-turnover.

Q. Where do baby apes sleep?

A. In an apricot.

Q. What sort of tools do you need to make mush-rooms?

A. Toads-tools.

Q. What would you be if you had jelly in one ear and custard in the other?

A. A trifle deaf.

## *Social Mechanism*

When people always
try to take

the very smallest
piece of cake

how can it also
always be
that that's the one
that's left for me?

*Piet Hein*

# *The Story of Augustus who would not have any Soup*

Augustus was a chubby lad;
Fat ruddy cheeks Augustus had;
And everybody saw with joy
The plump and hearty healthy boy.
He ate and drank as he was told,
And never let his soup get cold.
But one day, one cold winter's day,
He scream'd out – 'Take the soup away!
O take the nasty soup away!
I won't have any soup to-day.'

Next day, now look, the picture shows
How lank and lean Augustus grows!
Yet, though he feels so weak and ill,
The naughty fellow cries out still –
'Not any soup for me, I say:
O take the nasty soup away;
I won't have any soup to-day.'

The third day comes; oh what a sin!
To make himself so pale and thin.
Yet, when the soup is put on table,
He screams, as loud as he is able, –
'Not any soup for me. I say:
O take the nasty soup away!
I won't have any soup to-day.'

Look at him, now the fourth day's come!
He scarcely weighs a sugar-plum;
He's like a little bit of thread,
And on the fifth day, he was – dead!

*Heinrich Hoffman*

## *from* The Babees' Book

Now must I tell you shortly what you shall do at noon when your lord goes to his meat. Be ready to fetch him clear water, and hold the towel for him until he has done, and leave not until he be set down, and ye have heard grace said. Stand before him until he bids you sit, and be always ready to serve him with clean hands.

When ye be set, keep your own knife clean and sharp, that so ye may carve honestly your own meat.

Let courtesy and silence dwell with you, and tell no foul tales to another.

Cut your bread with your knife and break it not. Lay a clean trencher before you, and when your pottage is brought, take your spoon and eat quietly; and do not leave your spoon in the dish, I pray you.

Look ye be not caught leaning on the table, and keep clear of soiling the cloth.

Do not hang your head over your dish, or in any wise drink with full mouth.

Keep from picking your nose, your teeth, your nails at meal-time – so we are taught.

Advise you against taking so muckle meat into your mouth but that ye may right well answer when men speak to you.

When ye shall drink, wipe your mouth clean with a cloth, and your hands also, so that you shall not in any way soil the cup, for then shall none of your companions be loth to drink with you.

Likewise, do not touch the salt in the salt-cellar with any meat; but lay salt honestly on your trencher, for that is courtesy.

Do not carry your knife to your mouth with food, or hold the meat with your hands in any wise; and also if divers goodmeats are brought to you, look that with all courtesy ye assay of each; and if your dish be taken away with its meat and another brought, courtesy demands that ye shall let it go and not ask for it back again.

And if strangers be set at table with you, and savoury meat be brought or sent to you, make them good cheer with part of it, for certainly it is not polite when others be present at meat with you, to keep all that is brought you, and like churls vouchsafe nothing to others.

Do not cut your meat like field-men who have such an appetite that they reck not in what wise, where or when or how ungoodly they hack at their meat; but, sweet children, have always your delight in courtesy and in gentleness, and eschew boisterousness with all your might.

When cheese is brought, have a clean trencher, on which with a clean knife ye may cut it; and in your feeding look ye appear goodly, and keep your tongue from jangling, for so indeed shall ye deserve a name for gentleness and good governance, and always advance yourself in virtue.

When the end of the meal is come, clean your knives, and look you put them up where they ought to be, and keep your seat until you have washed, for so wills honesty.

When ye have done, look then that ye rise up without laughter or joking or boisterous word and go to your lord's table, and there stand, and pass not from him until grace be said and brought to an end.

*(This comes from a medieval handbook of etiquette, written about 1475 for young princes, probably for those princes, Edward V and Richard, Duke of York, who were murdered in the Tower.)*

## *Humpty Dumpty's 'Eggy Song'*

It's a very hard life for a poor old egg
With only a delicate shell.
For people don't see
How cruel they can be
And they never treat an egg-head well.

They crack eggy jokes, and think it's such fun
To see just how far they can go,
They couldn't care less
If we end up in a mess,
They're a hard-boiled lot, you know.

To them it's so smart to make fowl remarks
And say just eggsactly what they feel,
It's strictly for the birds
What they do with their words,
They seem to forget that I'm real.

The most bird-brained have some jokes they must make,
A pun or a riddle to try,
Each one's an eggspert,
They don't intend to hurt,
– They just wonder if I'll scramble, poach or fry.

Use your own secret eggy language. It's very simple – there are only two rules. All you have to do is to put the word 'egg' before every vowel in every word, and to add an 'e' to every word that ends with an 'e'.

So, 'Hello' becomes 'Heggelleggo' and 'Goodbye' turns into 'Geggoeggodbyeggee'.

Now here is an eggy sentence for you to de-code:

DEGGID YEGGOEGGU KNEGGOW THEGGAT EGGIT TEGGAKEGGES FEGGORTY MEGGIN-EGGUTEGGES TEGGO BEGGOEGGIL THEGGEE EGGEGG EGGOF EGGAN EGGOSTREGGICH?

## *The Pig*

The pig exclaimed, on seeing the slicer,
'I think this world might well be nicer –

Which of us, should a vote be taken,
Would want to finish up as bacon?'

The slicer rasped, 'Now listen, pig!
Your brains are small; your bottom's big

This world is full of woe and waste –
Be grateful you're to someone's taste!'

*Edward Lucie-Smith*

## BRAIN BOTHER

If a white chaff eats more than a white chiff, and a black chaff eats more than a white chaff, and a black chaff eats less than a black chiff, which is the cheapest to feed?

A white chiff

# Make Yourself Food from Flowers

## Elderflower Fritters

*You will need*
25 white elderflower clusters
salt
fat for frying
icing sugar

*For the batter*
100 g plain flour
2 eggs
250 ml milk
½ teaspoon salt
1 teaspoon melted butter

Wash the flower clusters in a large bowl of cold, salted water. Remove the stems and leaves without breaking the clusters. Drain the flowers on kitchen paper.

Make the batter by sieving the flour into a bowl, making a well in the centre and breaking the eggs into it. Stir with a wooden spoon, adding the milk a little at a time. Add the salt and butter and beat until smooth and creamy. Dip each flower cluster into the batter and fry in deep hot fat until golden brown, taking great care not to splash the fat. Sprinkle with icing sugar and serve hot.

# *Betty Botter*

Betty Botter
bought some butter,
But, she said,
the butter's bitter.
If I put it
in my batter,
It will make
my batter bitter.
But a bit
of better butter –
That would make
my batter better.
So she bought
a bit of butter,
Better than
her bitter butter.
And she put it
in her batter,
And the batter
was not bitter.
So 'twas better
Betty Botter
Bought a bit
of better butter.

# FASCINATING FACT

Did you know that:

The largest dish in the world is roast camel? It is often eaten as a speciality at Bedouin weddings. The camel is roasted whole, and inside it is a roasted sheep. The roasted sheep is stuffed with chickens; the chickens are stuffed with fish; and the fish are stuffed with eggs. Sounds delicious.

## *from* New England Farmer, 1824

We once heard of a traveller who told a story of an immense pie – so large, indeed, that after the crust and meat were eaten, a dozen couples danced in the dish, and one of them lost a buckle in the gravy. Now we cannot boast that Sheffield has ever produced such a pie, but one was exhibited and eaten at Mr Turner's on Christmas Eve, of the following size – one yard and a half long, two feet wide, one foot deep, ten feet round. It was baked by Mr Barlow, quite perfect; the crust consisting of six stone of rye meal.

## Chinese Proverb

When you have only two pennies left in the world, buy a loaf of bread with one, and a lily with the other.

## *Moonlit Apples*

At the top of the house the apples are laid in rows,
And the skylight lets the moonlight in, and those
Apples are deep-sea apples of green. There goes
A cloud on the moon in the autumn night.

A mouse in the wainscot scratches, and scratches, and then
There is no sound at the top of the house of men
Or mice; and the cloud is blown, and the moon again
Dapples the apples with deep-sea light.

They are lying in rows there, under the gloomy beams;
On the sagging floor; they gather the silver streams
Out of the moon, those moonlit apples of dreams,
And quiet is the steep stair under.

In the corridors under there is nothing but sleep,
And stiller than ever on orchard boughs they keep
Tryst with the moon, and deep is the silence, deep
On moon-washed apples of wonder.

*John Drinkwater*

## FAMOUS FALLACY

Although we always think that the fruit Eve used to tempt Adam in the Garden of Eden was an apple, the Bible doesn't say what it was. It could have been a fig.

# *Wanted*

I want a kitchen-garden
With box to line the routes,
Where things get soft and harden
And cling to people's boots;
I want dark earth to dibble
And Brussels-sprouts in droves
And hazy days to nibble
Among the gooseberry groves.

I want to be imprisoned
By peach-pervaded wall,
With Quarendens wind-wizened
And beet at beck and call,
With marrows growing grosser
And pumpkins past their prime
And gardeners saying 'No, Sir,'
And 'Yes, Sir,' all the time.

I want to be surrounded
By bone-manure and bees,
With broccoli unbounded
And rhubarb to the knees,
With spinach in the making
And onions up in bed
And Pippin-blossom breaking
Into the potting-shed.

I want to have peas podded
And cabbage neatly patched;
I want my figs home-prodded,
My apricots attached;
I want plums free from custard
And leisure to express
Myself with more than mustard
And, if it's coming, cress.

*Daniel Pettiward*

## *from* Of Gardens

And because the breath of flowers is far sweeter in the air – where it comes and goes, like the warbling of music – than in the hand, therefore nothing is more fit for that delight, than to know what be the flowers and plants that do best perfume the air.

That which above all others yields the sweetest smell in the air, is the violet, which comes twice a year; about the middle of April, and about Bartholomewtide. Next to that is the musk-rose. Then the strawberry-leaves dying, which yield a most excellent cordial smell. Then the flower of the vines; it is a little dust which grows upon the cluster in the first coming forth. Then sweet-briar. Then wall-flowers, which are very delightful to be set under a parlour or low chamber window. Then pinks and gillyflowers, specially the matted pink and clove gillyflower. Then the flowers of the lime-tree. Then the honeysuckles, so they be somewhat afar off.

But those which perfume the air most delightfully, not passed by as the rest, but being trodden upon and crushed, are three: that is, burnet, wild thyme, and water-mints. Therefore you are to set whole alleys of them, to have the pleasure when you walk or tread.

*Francis Bacon*

# RIDICULOUS RIDDLES

Q. How do you stop moles digging up the garden?

A. Hide their spades.

Q. Why did the window-box?

A. Because it saw the garden fence.

Q. How do you catch a rabbit?

A. Go behind a tree and make a noise like a lettuce.

First I am as white as snow,
Then as green as grass I grow,
Next I am as red as blood,
Lastly I'm as black as mud.
What am I?

A Bramble

## *The Flower-cart Man*

When it's just past April
And going on May,
The bent old Flower Man
Comes our way.

His clothes are very baggy,
His horse is lean and gray.
But, like a walking garden,
His cart with plants is gay.

All filled with nodding rose trees
To make your parlour bright,
With tulips for your table,
Or daisies gold and bright.

With pansy plants and lilies,
Primrose and daffodil,
And red geraniums in pots
To trim your window sill.

Everywhere his cart goes
The air smells sweet,
As the gray horse and he
Jog from street to street.

They say that Spring's a lady
And it may be so,
Though she never stopped on our street
As far as I know –

But the bent old Flower Man
Comes our way,
When it's just past April
And going on May.

*Rachel Field*

## *My Aunt*

You've heard how a green thumb
Makes flowers come
Quite without toil
Out of any old soil.

Well, my Aunt's thumbs were green.
At a touch, she had blooms
Of prize Chrysanthemums –
The grandest ever seen.

People from miles around
Came to see those flowers
And were truly astounded
By her unusual powers.

One day a little weed
Pushed up to drink and feed
Among the pampered flowers
At her water-can showers.

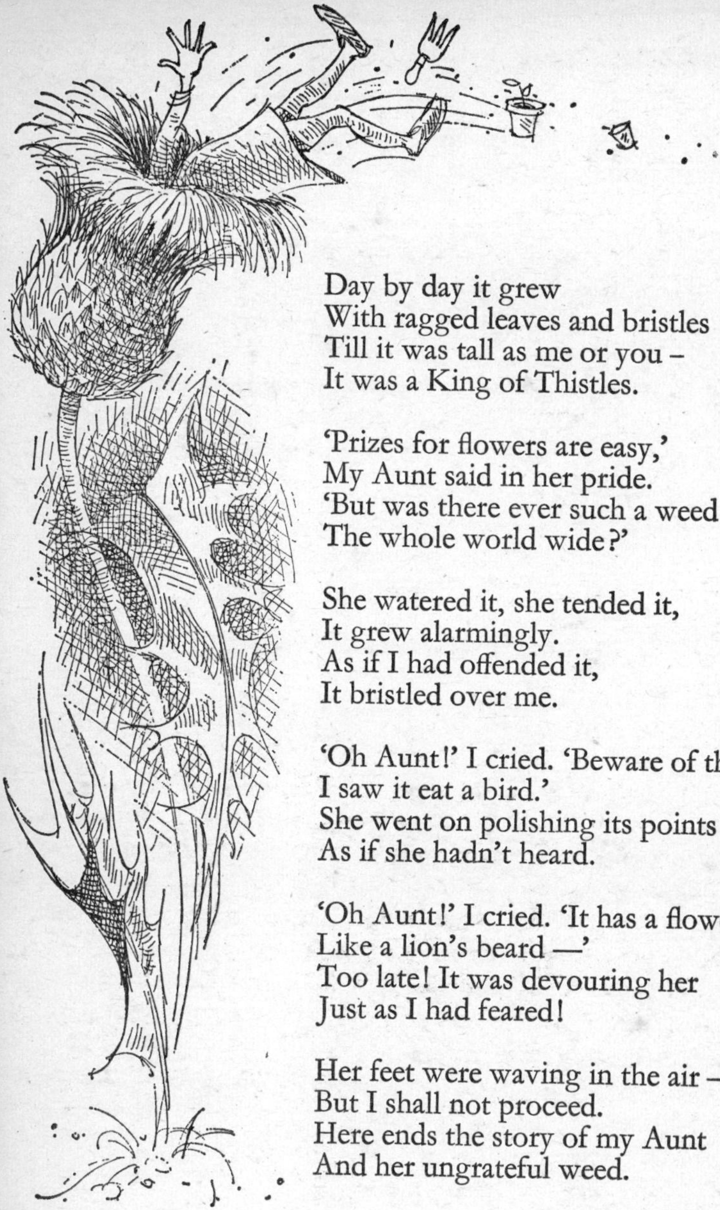

Day by day it grew
With ragged leaves and bristles
Till it was tall as me or you –
It was a King of Thistles.

'Prizes for flowers are easy,'
My Aunt said in her pride.
'But was there ever such a weed
The whole world wide?'

She watered it, she tended it,
It grew alarmingly.
As if I had offended it,
It bristled over me.

'Oh Aunt!' I cried. 'Beware of that!
I saw it eat a bird.'
She went on polishing its points
As if she hadn't heard.

'Oh Aunt!' I cried. 'It has a flower
Like a lion's beard —'
Too late! It was devouring her
Just as I had feared!

Her feet were waving in the air –
But I shall not proceed.
Here ends the story of my Aunt
And her ungrateful weed.

*Ted Hughes*

## *from* The Country Child

Every day she had this ordeal, a walk of a mile or more through the dense old wood, along the deserted footpath. A hundred years ago, before the highway was made, it was a well-worn road between the villages of Raddle and distant Mellow. Now it only went to Windystone Hall, and everyone walked or drove along the turnpike by the river, deep in the valley, two hundred feet below.

No one ever knew Susan's fears, she never even formulated them to herself, except as 'things'. But whether they were giants which she half expected to see straddle out of the dark distance, or dwarfs, hidden behind the trees, or bears and Indians in the undergrowth, or even the trees themselves marching down upon her, she was not certain. They must never be mentioned, and, above all, They must never know she was afraid.

It was no use for her to tell herself there were no giants, or that bears had disappeared in England centuries ago, or that trees could not walk. She knew that quite well, but the terror remained, a subconscious fear which quickly rose to consciousness when she pressed back the catch of the gate at the entrance to the wood, and closed it soundlessly, as she entered the deep listening wood on her way home from school in the dusky evenings.

In the middle of Dark Wood the climbing path rose up a steep incline, too steep for Susan to hurry, with black shadows on either side. Then it skirted a field, a small, queer, haunted-looking field of ragwort and bracken, long given to the wild wood, which pressed in on every side. A high rudely-made wall surrounded it, through the chinks of which she was sure that eyes were watching. To pass this field was the culmination of agony, for she had to walk close to the wall in the semi-darkness of overhanging trees, and nothing could save her if a long arm and skinny hand shot out.

At the top of the field, which sloped up the wood, was a tumbledown building, which was the authentic House that Jack built, with rats and malt complete, but long ago it had been deserted and now Fear lived there. Once she saw a battered man creeping through the bracken towards the ruin, but he never saw the little shadow with a school bag on her back slip past the mossy gate of the field.

Beyond the ragwort field was a fair open stretch of wood, with cow-wheat and delicate fumitory growing by the path. The trees were not so close together, and a glimpse of the blue sky came through in summer, or a star in the winter.

The child's heart ceased its heavy pounding and she took in deep breaths in readiness for the next ordeal, an immense rugged oak tree which waited at the cross-road, where her path cut across two others. One way led downhill to a cottage in the fields below the wood, a path no one used. The other went up the steep sides of the wood past great boulders which lay among the trees like primitivc beasts crouching in the dark, until it faded away to nothing in the bracken.

But something was behind the oak tree, hidden, lurking, and the leaves all watched her approach. She threw back her head and stared boldly at it, but her feet were winged for flight as she slipped softly along. Once, two years ago, when she was seven, a pair of eyes had looked at her from behind the tree, and once a dead white cow had lain there, swollen and stiff, brought to be buried in the wood.

A nut tree stood in her path, low, human, but it was friendly, and always she touched its branches with fluttering trembling fingers, receiving solace from the warm twigs, as she passed on to meet the oak. She held her head sideways, pretending to look up at the scrap of sky, but her eyes were peeping behind, like a scared rabbit's, and the tree seemed to turn its branches and look after her, whilst the thing, whatever it was, skipped round the trunk to the other side. She never turned to look behind her, but trusted to her sense of hearing, which had become very acute with the strain imposed upon it. She whispered a little prayer, a cry to God for help, as she left the tree behind.

Then she walked down the tunnel of beech trees, for the oaks were left behind and the character of the wood had changed. The trees thinned and the beeches rose clear of undergrowth with massive smooth grey trunks from the carpet of golden leaves. Susan breathed naturally again, and walked rapidly forward, heeding neither rock nor tree, her eager eyes fixed on the light ahead. The evening sunshine streamed through the end of the path, a circle of radiance, where a stile and broken gate ended the wood.

*Alison Uttley*

Which of these two parallel lines is the longer?

## Make a Small Fat Hairy Friend

Take a cream or yogurt carton, scrub it quite clean, and dry it. Paint a funny face on one side of the carton. Fill the carton right to the top with damp soil. Scatter a sprinkling of grass seed on the soil.

Within a few days your friend will have grown a mop of green grass hair. Water your Green-Haired Gregory whenever the soil gets too dry, and cut his hair whenever it gets too long.

YOGURT
Grass Seed

There was an Old Man of Dundee,
Who frequented the top of a tree;
When disturbed by the crows,
He abruptly arose,
And exclaimed, 'I'll return to Dundee!'

A colonel called out with great force
In the midst of Hyde Park for a horse.
All the soldiers looked round –
But none could be found:
So he just rhododendron. Of course!

There was a young farmer of Leeds
Who swallowed six packets of seeds.
It soon came to pass
He was covered with grass,
And he couldn't sit down for the weeds.

*Sowing Beans*

One for the mouse, one for the crow,
One to rot, one to grow.

## FASCINATING FACT

Did you know that:

Jumping beans jump because they have live fleas inside them?

## TONGUE TWISTER

A proper crop of poppies is a proper poppy crop.

# FASCINATING FACT

Did you know that:

When a woman from Norfolk, England, complained to her dentist that she had a sore mouth he examined her, and discovered that a healthy young tomato plant was growing under her false teeth?

# BRAIN BOTHERER

A farmer put nine ears of corn in a box, where it was discovered by a mouse. Each day, the mouse carried away three ears, yet it took him nine days to carry off all the corn. Why?

He only took one ear of corn each day – the other two were his own ears.

## *from* Ecclesiastes

To everything there is a season, and a time to every purpose under the heaven;
A time to be born, and a time to die; a time to plant, and a time to pluck up that which is planted;
A time to kill, and a time to heal; a time to break down, and a time to build up;
A time to weep, and a time to laugh; a time to mourn, and a time to dance;
A time to keep, and a time to cast away; a time to keep silence, and a time to speak;
A time to love, and a time to hate; a time of war, and a time of peace.

## *Solomon Grundy*

Solomon Grundy,
Born on a Monday,
Christened on Tuesday,
Married on Wednesday,
Took ill on Thursday,
Worse on Friday,
Died on Saturday,
Buried on Sunday:
That is the end
Of Solomon Grundy.

# Good Friday, 1802

When I undrew my curtains in the morning, I was much affected by the beauty of the prospect and the change. The sun shone, the wind had passed away, the hills looked cheerful, the river was very bright as it flowed into the lake. The church rises up behind a little knot of rocks, the steeple not so high as an ordinary three-storey house. Trees, in a row in the garden under the wall. After William had shaved we set forward. The valley is at first broken by little rocky woody knolls that make retiring places, fairy valleys in the vale, the river winds along under these hills travelling not in a bustle but not slowly to the lake. We saw a fisherman in the flat meadow on the other side of the water. He came towards us and threw his line over the two-arched bridge.

A sheep came plunging through the river, stumbled up the bank and passed close to us, it had been frightened by an insignificant little dog on the other side, its fleece dropped a glittering shower under its belly. Primroses by the roadside, pile wort that shone like stars of gold in the sun, violets, strawberries, retired and half buried among the grass. When we came to the foot of Brothers Water I left William sitting on the bridge and went along the path on the right side of the lake through the wood. I was delighted with what I saw. The water under the boughs of the bare old trees, the simplicity of the mountains and the exquisite beauty of the path. There was one grey cottage. I hung over the gate, and thought I could have stayed for ever.

When I returned I found William writing a poem descriptive of the sights we saw and heard. There was the gentle flowing of the stream, the glittering lively lake, green fields without a living creature to be seen on them, behind us, a flat pasture with forty-two cattle feeding, to our left the road leading to the hamlet, no smoke there, the sun shone on the bare roofs. The people were at work ploughing, harrowing and sowing – lasses spreading dung, a dog's barking now and then, cocks crowing, birds twittering, the snow in patches at the top of the highest hills, yellow palms, purple and green twigs on the birches, ashes with their glittering spikes quite bare.

*Dorothy Wordsworth*

## *The Cock is Crowing*

(Written in March, while resting on the bridge
at the foot of BrothersWater)

The cock is crowing,
The stream is flowing,
The small birds twitter,
The lake doth glitter,
The green field sleeps in the sun;
The oldest and youngest
Are at work with the strongest;
The cattle are grazing,
Their heads never raising;
There are forty feeding like one!

Like an army defeated
The snow hath retreated,
And now doth fare ill
On the top of the bare hill;
The Ploughboy is whooping – anon – anon:
There's joy in the mountains;
There's life in the fountains;
Small clouds are sailing,
Blue sky prevailing;
The rain is over and gone!

*William Wordsworth*

# RIDICULOUS RIDDLES

Q. What time is it when an elephant sits on a fence?

A. Time to get a new fence.

Q. If a man smashed a clock, could he be accused of killing time?

A. Not if the clock struck first.

Q. I occur once in every minute, twice in every moment, but not once in a hundred thousand years. What am I?

A. The letter 'm'.

## *from* The Eve of St Agnes

St Agnes' Eve – Ah, bitter chill it was!
The owl, for all his feathers, was a-cold;
The hare limp'd trembling through the frozen grass,
And silent was the flock in woolly fold.

*John Keats*

# FAMOUS FALLACY

Did you know that:

The twentieth century didn't begin on January 1st 1900, but on January 1st 1901?

## *A Child's Calendar*

Monday's child is fair of face,
Tuesday's child is full of grace,
Wednesday's child is full of woe,
Thursday's child has far to go,
Friday's child is loving and giving,
Saturday's child works hard for its living,
And the child that is born on the Sabbath day
Is bonny and blithe, and good and gay.

Thirty days hath September,
April, June and November;
All the rest have thirty-one,
Excepting February alone,
Which has twenty-eight days clear
And twenty-nine in each leap-year.

## *Pancake Day Rhyme*

Tippety tippety tin
Give me a pancake and I will come in.
Tippety tippety toe,
Give me a pancake and I will go.

## *Pace-egg Song*

for Easter Day

Now we're jolly pace-eggers all in one round,
We've come a-pace-egging, we hope you'll prove kind;
We hope you'll prove kind with your eggs and strong beer
For we'll come no more near you until the next year.
Fol de diddle ol, fol de dee, fol de diddle and dum day.

Now ladies and gentlemen who sit by the fire
Put your hands in your pockets, that's all we desire.
Put your hands in your pockets and pull out your purse,
And give us a trifle, you won't feel much worse.
Fol de diddle ol, fol de dee, fol de diddle ol dum day.

## *Soul-cake Song*

for All Hallows Day

Soul! Soul! a soul-cake!
Please, good missus, a soul-cake!
An apple, a pear, a plum or a cherry,
Or any good thing to make us merry.
One for Peter, two for Paul,
And three for He who made us all.

## *Bright Celery*

for Christmas

Now Christmas is here
Let's have a drop of beer,
Bright celery, bright celery,
And a happy New Year.
Apples to eat, and nuts to crack,
Here we come with our rat-a-tat-tat.

Sneeze on Monday, sneeze for danger;
Sneeze on Tuesday, kiss a stranger;
Sneeze on Wednesday, get a letter;
Sneeze on Thursday, something better;
Sneeze on Friday, sneeze for sorrow;
Sneeze on Saturday, see your true love tomorrow.

## Birth Stones and Flowers

| | STONE | FLOWER |
|---|---|---|
| *January* | Garnet | Carnation |
| *February* | Amethyst | Violet |
| *March* | Bloodstone | Jonquil |
| *April* | Diamond | Sweet Pea |
| *May* | Emerald | Lily of the Valley |
| *June* | Agate | Rose |
| *July* | Ruby | Larkspur |
| *August* | Sardonyx | Gladioli |
| *September* | Sapphire | Aster |
| *October* | Opal | Calendula |
| *November* | Topaz | Chrysanthemum |
| *December* | Turquoise | Narcissus |

## TONGUE TWISTER

Does the wristwatch shop shut soon?

# BRAIN BOTHER

John and Sally go swimming, but they forget to take off their wristwatches, which are not waterproof. Consequently, Sally's stops, and refuses to start again, while John's begins to gain thirty seconds a day. If they do not alter their watches or have them mended, whose will tell the correct time more often?

Sally's will tell the right time twice a day. John's will tell the right time again after it has gained twelve hours. Since there are 43,200 seconds in twelve hours it will take it 1440 days.

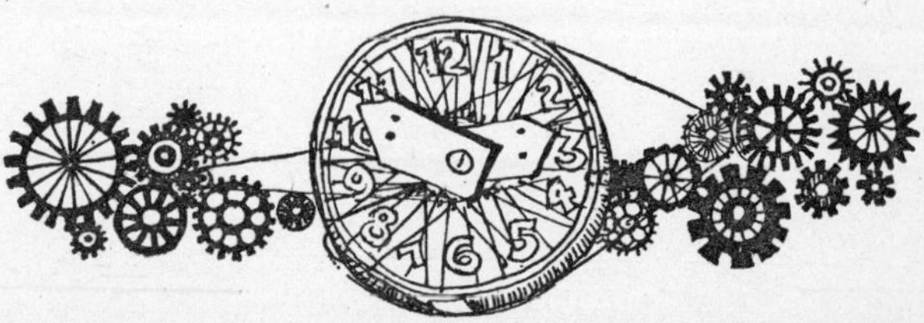

# FASCINATING FACT

Did you know that:

In a village in Wiltshire in England there is a church clock made from old bedsteads, bicycles and pram frames. It is in perfect working order, and keeps perfect time.

## Something to Do

Measure the speed of your reactions. All you need is a ruler, and a friend to help you.

Lean your arm on a table, with your hand over the edge. Ask your friend to hold the ruler with the bottom end, showing the nought centimetre mark, just between and level with your open finger and thumb.

Then, whenever he likes, and giving you no warning, he must drop the ruler, and you must close your finger and thumb to catch it as quickly as you possibly can.

Look at the ruler and read the centimetre mark nearest your thumb and you'll see how far the ruler has fallen.

Now look at this printed table and see how good your reactions are. You can use it to test your friends too.

**Reaction Time Table**

| *Number of centimetres the ruler falls* | *Reaction time in hundredths of a second* | *Rating* |
|---|---|---|
| 2 | 7 | Excellent |
| 4 | 9 | |
| 6 | 11 | Very Good |
| 8 | 13 | |
| 10 | 14 | |
| 12 | 16 | Good |
| 14 | 17 | |
| 16 | 18 | |
| 18 | 19 | |
| 20 | 20 | Fair |
| 22 | 21 | |
| 24 | 22 | |
| 26 | 23 | Poor |
| 28 | 24 | |
| 30 | 25 | |

## *from* Borrobil

The three of them settled down in their hiding-place, Borrobil and Jean on one side of the stone, Donald on the other. And scarcely had they settled down than they heard the sound of a horn. It was blown three times. And riding into the Ring from the east came two heralds on white horses.

'The heralds of Summer,' whispered Borrobil. 'Warm Wind and Gentle Rain. Always do they ride before the White King to announce his coming.'

The heralds rode round the Ring. Again they blew their horns. And in from the east rode the White King of Summer. He, too, rode a white steed; his armour was of gold, his shield was a bright blue, and his helmet seemed to be crowned with a wreath of green leaves. And as he rode into the Ring so his heralds turned and rode out to the east again, there taking up their stand outside the Ring by the very stones through which the King had come.

'The White King rides a white horse,' whispered Borrobil. 'His armour is of gold, for gold is the summer corn; his shield is bright blue, for bright blue is the summer sky; and his crest is a sprig of the green oak leaves.'

The White King rode proudly round the Ring. He turned, and rode to its very centre. There he reined in his steed, and lifting his sword on high called out in a loud voice – 'Hear, O Black King of Winter, defender in this combat. Appear forthwith to defend thyself and thy rule against the White King of Summer who hath come to meet thee.'

There was no answer. Again the White King rode proudly round the Ring. Again he rode to its very centre. Again he called forth his challenge, and this time he ended with the words – 'The day passeth; therefore come without delay.'

Still there was no answer. Once more the White King rode proudly round the Ring. Once more he rode to its very centre. Once more he called forth his challenge, and this time he ended with the words – 'Appear in haste; for the day is wellnigh spent. Appear if thou wouldst maintain thyself within this land. Appear to defend thy rule before the sun goeth down.'

And with that the White King turned his horse and rode to the eastern side of the Ring.

Then, even as the White King reached the side of the Ring and turned again, there to take up his stand facing the centre of the Ring, so, from the west, came the sound of a horn. It was blown three times. And riding into the Ring from the western side came two heralds on black horses.

'The heralds of Winter,' whispered Borrobil. 'Bitter Frost and Raging Storm. Always do they ride before the Black King to announce his coming.'

Again the heralds of Winter blew their horns, and in from the west rode the Black King. He, too, rode a black steed; his armour was red rust; his shield was dull and dark; and his helmet was crowned with white. And as he rode into the Ring so his heralds turned and rode out to the west again, there taking up their stand outside the Ring by the very stones through which the king had come.

'The Black King rides a black horse,' whispered Borrobil. 'His armour is of the red rust that eats and gnaws; his shield is dull and dark as the days of his rule; and his crest is the white frost that he lays over all the land.

Straight to the centre of the Ring rode the Black King. There he reined in his horse, and lifting his sword on high called out in a loud voice:

'Who would drive me from the land?
Here let him stand.
Here let him strike with all his might,
Ere day be night.'

And the Black King turned his horse and rode to the western side of the Ring, there to take up his stand.

And now the White King once more rode to the centre of the Ring. He in turn held high his sword and called out in a firm voice:

'Here I stand;
'Tis I shall drive Black Winter from the land.
'Tis I shall drive him forth in headlong flight.
Ere day be night.'

The White King brandished his sword, and holding his horse firm on the rein stayed in the very centre of the Ring. Then from the western side the Black King spurred his horse and rode to meet him. In the centre of the Ring they met. In the centre of the Ring their swords crossed.

The Black King pressed in, hard and furious. His onslaught was like the winter's gale that would bear all down before it. Thick and fast fell his blows, and as they fell they seemed to strike sunbeams and sunlight from the White King's armour. But despite the fury of the onslaught, still the White King stood fast. Then, once, the Black King paused as though his fury had outspent itself. And as he paused, so the White King bore down upon him. His own sword fell hard and true upon the Black King's helm. Snow and ice were scattered around. Still the White King struck hard and oft. The Black King sank low within his saddle. He swayed. He seemed about to fall. But, making one last effort, he regained his seat, and turning his steed, galloped madly in headlong flight towards the western side of the Ring, and so out towards the lowering sun.

Through the dark network of trees the sun seemed to be balancing like a fiery ball upon the edge of the distant land. For one brief moment that fiery ball blazed round and full; with the next moment, as the Black King galloped madly from the Ring, the fiery ball had gone. And even as Borrobil had warned the children, so, with the sinking of the sun, they passed at once from the bright light of day to the blackness of night.

*William Croft Dickinson*

There was a young fellow of Perth,
Who was born on the day of his birth;
He was married, they say,
On his wife's wedding day,
And he died when he quitted the earth.

There was a young fellow named Hall,
Who fell in the spring in the fall;
'Twould have been a sad thing
If he'd died in the spring,
But he didn't – he died in the fall.

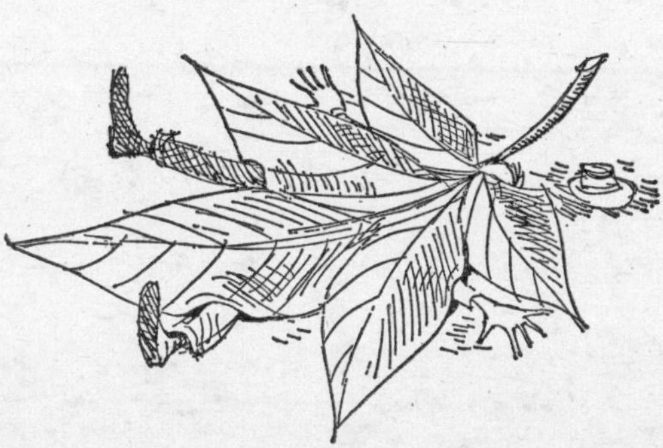

There was a young woman named Bright,
Whose speed was much faster than light,
She set out one day
In a relative way,
And returned on the previous night.

## *Little Things*

Little things that run and fail
And die in silence and despair.
Little things that fight and fail and fall
On earth and sea and air.
All trapt and frightened little things
The Mouse, the Coney, hear our prayer.
As we forgive those done to us
The Lamb, the Linnet and the Hare
Forgive us all our trespasses
Little creatures everywhere.

*James Stephens*

## *The Wish*

I wish I was a little grub
With whiskers round my tummy
I'd climb into a honey-pot
And make my tummy gummy.

## *from* My Family and Other Animals

One day I found a fat female scorpion in the wall, wearing what at first glance appeared to be a pale fawn fur coat. Closer inspection proved that this strange garment was made up of a mass of tiny babies clinging to the mother's back. I was enraptured by this family, and I made up my mind to smuggle them into the house and up to my bedroom so that I might keep them and watch them grow up. With infinite care I manoeuvred the mother and family into a matchbox, and then hurried to the villa. It was rather unfortunate that just as I entered the door lunch should be served; however, I placed the matchbox carefully on the mantelpiece in the drawing-room, so that the scorpions should get plenty of air, and made my way to the dining-room and joined the family for the meal. Dawdling over my food, feeding Roger surreptitiously under the table and listening to the family arguing, I completely forgot about my exciting new captures. At last Larry, having finished, fetched the cigarettes from the drawing-room, and lying back in his chair he put one in his mouth and picked up the matchbox he had brought. Oblivious of my impending doom I watched him interestedly as, still talking glibly, he opened the matchbox.

Now I maintain to this day that the female scorpion meant no harm. She was agitated and a trifle annoyed at being shut up in a matchbox for so long, and so she seized the first opportunity to escape. She hoisted herself out of the box with great rapidity, her babies clinging on desperately, and scuttled on to the back of Larry's hand. There, not quite certain what to do next, she paused, her sting curved up at the ready. Larry, feeling the movement of her claws, glanced down to see what it was, and from that moment things got increasingly confused.

He uttered a roar of fright that made Lugaretzia drop a plate and brought Roger out from beneath the table, barking wildly. With a flick of his hand he sent the unfortunate scorpion flying down the table, and she landed midway between Margo and Leslie, scattering babies like confetti as she thumped on the cloth. Thoroughly enraged at this treatment, the creature sped towards Leslie, her sting quivering with emotion. Leslie leapt to his feet, overturning his chair, and flicked out desperately with his napkin, sending the scorpion rolling across the cloth towards Margo, who promptly let out a scream that any railway engine would have been proud to produce. Mother, completely bewildered by this sudden and rapid change from peace to chaos, put on her glasses and peered down the table to see what was causing the pandemonium, and at that moment Margo, in a vain attempt to stop the scorpion's advance, hurled a glass of water at it. The shower missed the animal completely, but successfully drenched Mother, who, not being able to stand cold water, promptly lost her breath and sat gasping at the end of the table, unable even to protest. The scorpion had now gone to ground under Leslie's plate, while her babies swarmed wildly all over the table. Roger, mystified by the panic, but determined to do his share, ran round and round the room, barking hysterically.

'It's that bloody boy again . . .' bellowed Larry.

'Look out! Look out! They're coming!' screamed Margo.

'All we need is a book,' roared Leslie; 'don't panic, hit 'em with a book.'

'What on earth's the *matter* with you all?' Mother kept imploring, mopping her glasses.

'It's that bloody boy . . . he'll kill the lot of us . . . Look at the table . . . knee-deep in scorpions . . .'

'Quick . . . quick . . . do something . . . Look out, look out!'

'Stop screeching and get a book, for God's sake . . . You're worse than the dog . . . Shut *up*, Roger . . .'

'By the Grace of God I wasn't bitten . . .'

'Look out . . . there's another one . . . Quick . . . quick . . .'

'Oh, shut up and get me a book or something . . .'

'But *how* did the scorpions get on the table, dear?'

'That bloody boy . . . Every matchbox in the house is a deathtrap'.

'Look out, it's coming towards me . . . Quick, quick, do something . . .'

'Hit it with your knife . . . *your knife* . . . Go on, hit it . . .'

Since no one had bothered to explain things to him, Roger was under the mistaken impression that the family were being attacked, and that it was his duty to defend them. As Lugaretzia was the only stranger in the room, he came to the logical conclusion that she must be the responsible party, so he bit her in the ankle. This did not help matters very much.

By the time a certain amount of order had been restored, all the baby scorpions had hidden themselves under various plates and bits of cutlery. Eventually, after impassioned pleas on my part, backed up by Mother, Leslie's suggestion that the whole lot be slaughtered was quashed. While the family, still simmering with rage and fright, retired to the drawing-room, I spent half an hour rounding up the babies, picking them up in a teaspoon, and returning them to their mother's back. Then I carried them outside on a saucer and, with the utmost reluctance, released them on the garden wall. Roger and I went and spent the afternoon on the hill-side, for I felt it would be prudent to allow the family to have a siesta before seeing them again.

*Gerald Durrell*

The shortest poem in the English language

## *On the Antiquity of Microbes*

Adam
Had 'em.

## *Good Company*

I sleep in a room at the top of the house
With a flea, and a fly, and a soft-scratching mouse,
And a spider who hangs by a thread from the ceiling,
Who gives me each day such a curious feeling
When I watch him at work on the beautiful weave
Of his web that's so fine I can hardly believe
It won't all end up in such terrible tangles,
For he sways as he weaves, and spins as he dangles.
I cannot get up to that spider, I know,
And I hope he won't get down to me here below,
And yet when I wake in the chill morning air
I'd miss him if he were not still swinging there,
For I have in my room such good company,
There's him, and the mouse, and the fly, and the flea.

*Leonard Clark*

## *How to Address a Bat*

Arymouse, arymouse, fly over my head,
And you shall ha' a crust o' bread;
And when I brew and when I bake,
You shall ha' a piece of my wedding-cake.

# FAMOUS FALLACY

Did you know that:

Bats are *not* blind, they see perfectly well.

## *Mules*

On mules we find two legs behind,
And two we find before,
We stand behind before we find
What the two behind be for.
When we're behind the two behind
We find what these be for,
So stand before the two behind,
Behind the two before.

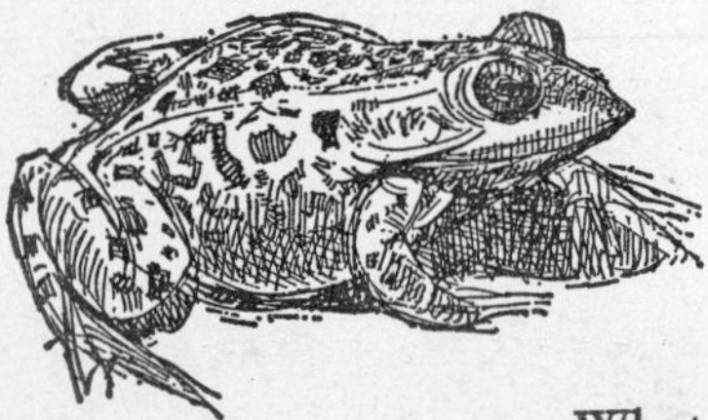

## *The Frog*

What a strange bird the frog are.
When he sit he stand almost;
When he jump he fly almost;
When he talk he cry almost;
He ain't got no sense hardly.
He ain't got no tail hardly, either.
He sit on what he ain't got almost.

# Beasts in Companies

A pride of lions.
A lepe of leopards.
A herd of harts, bucks and all sorts of deer.
A bevy of roes.
A sloth of bears.
A singular of boars.
A sownder of wild swine.
A dryft of tame swine.
A route of wolves.
A flock of sheep.
A tribe of goats.
A sculk of foxes.
A cete of badgers.
A richesse of martens.
A fesynes of ferrets.
A huske (or down) of hares.
A dule of turtle.
A nest of rabbits.
A harras of horses.
A rag of colts.
A stud of mares.
A pace of asses.
A baren of mules.
A drove of kine.
A clowder of cats.
A kendel of young cats.
A shrewdness of apes.
A labour of moles.
A mute of hounds.
A cowardice of curs.

## *The Serpent*

There was a serpent who had to sing.
There was. There was.
He simply gave up Serpenting.
Because. Because.
He didn't like his Kind of Life;
He couldn't find a proper Wife;
He was a Serpent with a soul;
He got no Pleasure down his Hole.
And so, of course, he had to Sing,
And Sing he did, like Anything!
The Birds, they were, they were Astounded;
And various Measures Propounded
To stop the Serpent's Awful Racket:
They bought a Drum. He wouldn't Whack it.

They sent – you always send – to Cuba
And got a Most Commodious Tuba;
They got a Horn, they got a Flute,
But Nothing would suit.
He said, 'Look, Birds, all this is futile:
I do *not* like to Bang or Tootle.'
And then he cut loose with a Horrible Note
That practically split the Top of his Throat.
'You see,' he said, with a Serpent's Leer,
'I'm Serious about my Singing Career!'
And the Woods Resounded with many a Shriek
As the Birds flew off to the End of Next Week.

*Theodore Roethke*

## TONGUE TWISTER

Six silent snakes slither slowly southward.

# FASCINATING FACT

Did you know that:
Serpents hear through their *jaws*?

## Make your own Singing Serpent

Find an old sock, and push your hand to the end of the foot. Move your fingers and thumb about until the toe of the sock looks like a mouth opening and closing.

Now cut two half-circles of red material, and sew or glue them into place to look like lips. On the part of the sock that is covering the back of your hand make two eyes by sewing into place two white circles and fastening black buttons on top. This is the snake's head.

Tuck in the heel of the sock and sew it down neatly. You can decorate the snake's body, if you want to, by sewing on buttons of all shapes, sizes and colours.

Practise using your serpent as a puppet by opening and closing your thumb and fingers and twisting your arm about while you sing with your own special serpent-voice.

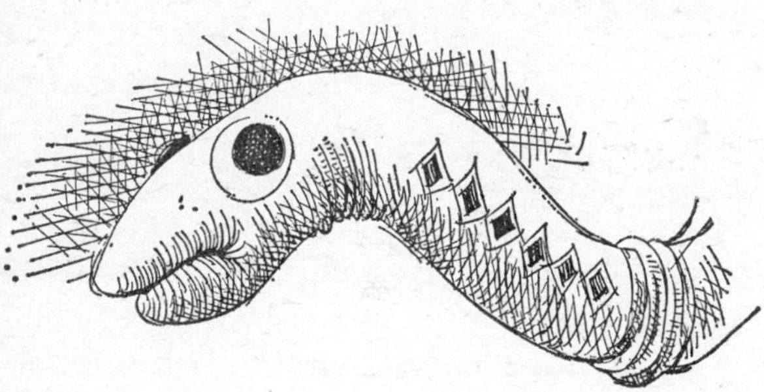

## *Toads*

A tree toad loved a she-toad
That lived up in a tree.
She was a three-toed tree toad,
But a two-toed toad was he.
The two-toed toad tried to win
The she-toad's friendly nod,
For the two-toed toad loved the ground
On which the three-toed toad trod.
But no matter how the two-toed tree toad tried,
He could not please her whim.
In her tree-toad bower,
With her three-toed power.
The she-toad vetoed him.

# RIDICULOUS RIDDLES

Q. What happened to the snake with a cold?

A. She adder viper nose.

Q. What do you get when you pour hot water down a rabbit hole?

A. Hot cross buns.

Q. Ten cats were sitting on a wall. One jumped down. How many were left?

A. None. They were all copy-cats.

# BRAIN BOTHERER

Persuade this matchstick fish to swim in the opposite direction by placing three of the matches in different positions.

*Answer on page 126*

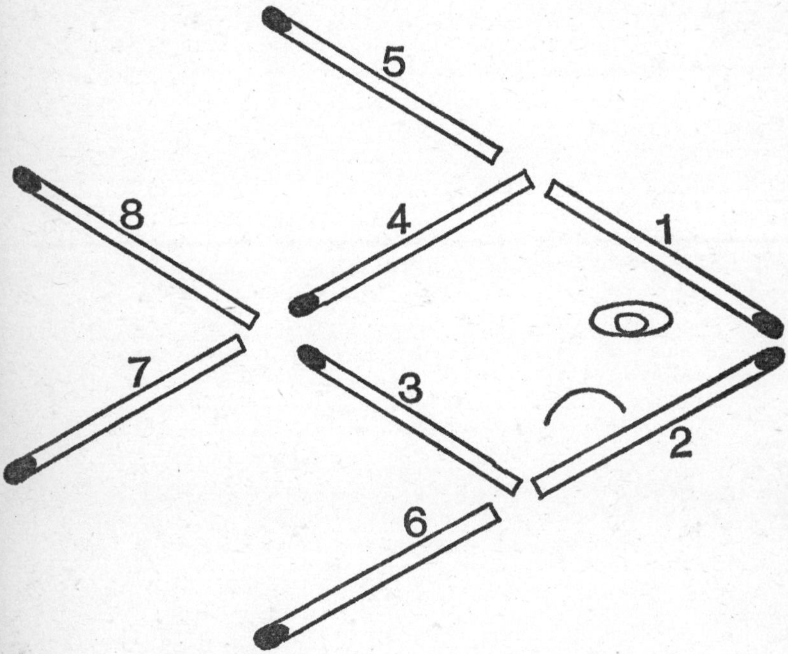


## *My Dog*

I've got a dog as thin as a rail,
He's got fleas all over his tail;
Every time his tail goes flop
The fleas at the bottom all jump to the top.

# *The Naming of Cats*

The Naming of Cats is a difficult matter,
It isn't just one of your holiday games;
You may think at first I'm as mad as a hatter
When I tell you, a cat must have *Three Different Names.*
First of all, there's the name that the family use daily,
Such as Peter, Augustus, Alonzo or James,
Such as Victor or Jonathan, George or Bill Bailey –
All of them sensible everyday names.
There are fancier names if you think they sound sweeter,
Some for the gentlemen, some for the dames:
Such as Plato, Admetus, Electra, Demeter –
But all of them sensible everyday names.
But I tell you, a cat needs a name that's particular,
A name that's peculiar, and more dignified,
Else how can he keep up his tail perpendicular,
Or spread out his whiskers, or cherish his pride?
Of names of this kind, I can give you a quorum,
Such as Munkustrap, Quaxo, or Coricopat,
Such as Bombalurina, or else Jellylorum –
Names that never belong to more than one cat.
But above and beyond there's still one name left over,
And that is the name that you never will guess;
The name that no human research can discover –
But *The Cat Himself Knows*, and will never confess.
When you notice a cat in profound meditation,
The reason, I tell you, is always the same:
His mind is engaged in a rapt contemplation
Of the thought, of the thought, of the thought of his name:
His ineffable effable
Effanineffable
Deep and inscrutable singular Name.

*T. S. Eliot*

There was a young lady named Maggie,
Whose dog was enormous and shaggy;
The front end of him
Looked vicious and grim –
But the back end was friendly and waggy.

Consider the poor hippopotamus:
His life is unduly monotonous.
He lives half asleep
At the edge of the deep,
And his face is as big as his bottom is.

There once were three owls in a wood
Who always sang hymns when they could:
What the words were about
One could never make out,
But one felt it was doing them good.

Take a good look at this picture.
One minute it's a duck – the next, it's a rabbit.

# *Birds in Companies*

A sege of herons and bitterns.
A herd of swans, cranes and curlews.
A dopping of sheldrakes.
A spring of teals.
A covert of coots.
A gaggle of geese.
A skein of geese (flying).
A bevy of quails.
A covey of partridges.
A congregation of plovers.
A walk (or wisp) of snipe.
A fall of woodcocks.
A murmuration of starlings.
An exaltation of larks.
A watch of nightingales.
A badelynge of ducks.
A sord (or sute) of mallards.
A muster of peacocks.
A flight of doves and swallows.
A building of rooks.
A brood of hens.
A host of sparrows.
A nye of pheasants.
A cast of hawks.
A plump of wildfowl.
A desert of lapwings.
A company of widgeon.
A chattering of choughs.

# *Ducks*

I.

From troubles of the world
I turn to ducks,
Beautiful comical things
Sleeping or curled
Their heads beneath white wings
By water cool,
Or finding curious things
To eat in various mucks
Beneath the pool,
Tails uppermost, or waddling
Sailor-like on the shores
Of ponds, or paddling
-Left! right!- with fanlike feet
Which are for steady oars
When they (white galleys) float
Each bird a boat
Rippling at will the sweet
Wide waterway . . .

When night is fallen *you* creep
Upstairs, but drakes and dillies
Nest with pale water-stars,
Moonbeams and shadow bars,
And water-lilies:
Fearful too much to sleep
Since they've no locks
To click against the teeth
Of weasel and fox.
And warm beneath
Are eggs of cloudy green
Whence hungry rats and lean
Would stealthily suck
New life, but for the mien,
The bold ferocious mien
Of the mother-duck.

2.

Yes, ducks are valiant things
On nests of twigs and straws,
And ducks are soothy things
And lovely on the lake
When that the sunlight draws
Thereon their pictures dim
In colours cool.
And when beneath the pool
They dabble, and when they swim
And make their rippling rings,
O ducks are beautiful things!

But ducks are comical things:–
As comical as you.
Quack!
They waddle round, they do.
They eat all sorts of things,
And then they quack.
By barn and stable and stack
They wander at their will,
But if you go too near
They look at you through black
Small topaz-tinted eyes
And wish you ill.
Triangular and clear
They leave their curious track
In mud at the water's edge,
And there amid the sedge
And slime they gobble and peer,
Saying "Quack! quack!"

3.

When God had finished the stars and whirl of coloured
  suns,
He turned His mind from big things to fashion little ones,
Beautiful tiny things (like daisies) He made, and then
He made the comical ones in case the minds of men
  Should stiffen and become
  Dull, humourless, and glum:
And so forgetful of their Maker be
As to take even themselves – *quite seriously*
Caterpillars and cats are lively and excellent puns:
All God's jokes are good – even the practical ones!
And as for the duck, I think God must have smiled a bit
Seeing those bright eyes blink on the day He fashioned it.
And He's probably laughing still at the sound that came
  out of its bill!

*F. W. Harvey*

## *Something to Crow about*

I sometimes think I'd rather crow
And be a rooster than to roost
And be a crow. But I dunno.

A rooster he can roost also,
Which don't seem fair when crows can't crow.
Which may help some. Still I dunno.

Crows should be glad of one thing though;
Nobody thinks of eating crow,
While roosters they are good enough
For anyone, unless they're tough.

There're lots of tough old roosters though,
And anyway a crow can't crow,
So mebby roosters stand more show.
It looks that way. But I dunno.

# Sky and Water

Look very carefully at this picture of birds and fish. You will see that in the middle the fish become sky if you look at the birds, and the birds become water if you concentrate on the fish. Like the magic boxes on page 101 they insist on changing places – you can't see both fish and birds together in this part of the picture.

# Magic Numbers

*Here is a sum:* 1000<br>20<br>30<br>1000<br>1030<br>1000<br>20<br>———<br>4100<br>———

Show this to your friend, but, to start with, cover up all the numbers except those in the top line with your hand. Then move your hand down so that he can see the next line and ask him to add it to the top line. Carry on in this way until he has added up all the numbers. He will almost certainly say that the total is 5000. Try it and see – it will trick people again and again.

**Now try this one:**
Ask a friend to write down the size of his shoes (no half sizes). Then he must double this figure, add 5, multiply by 5, then multiply by 10. To this he must add his age in years. Next, ask him to subtract 365, then add 115. If he's done his arithmetic properly the first figure or figures should show the size of his shoes, and the last should show his age.

**And finally . . .**
Ask him to multiply by 100 the number of the month in which he was born. Then ask him to add the number of the day of the month on which he was born. Now he must multiply the result by 2, add 8, multiply by 5, add 4, multiply by 10, then add another 4, and finally add his age. When he gives you his total you will be able to tell him his age and the date and month of his birthday. It will seem like magic to him, but in fact it's really very easy. All you have to do is subtract 444 from the number your friend has given you, and look at the result. The two right-hand figures will give you his age, the next two figures will give you the day of the month, and the left-hand figure or figures will give you the month.

## True and Wonderful

A discourse relating a strange and Monstrous Serpent or Dragon lately discovered, and yet living, to the great annoyance and divers slaughters both of men and cattle in Sussex, two miles from Horsham, in a wood called St Leonard's Forest, and thirty miles from London, this present month of August, 1641.

'In Sussex there is a pretty market towne called Horsham; near which is a forest, called St Leonard's Forest. And there, in a vast and unfrequented place; heathie; vaultie; full of unwholesome shades, and overgrown hollows; this serpent is thought to be bred. Certaine and too true it is that there it yet lives. And it hath been seen within half a mile of Horsham; a wonder no doubt most terrible and noisome to the inhabitants thereabouts.

There is always in his tracke or path a glutinous and slimie matter, which is very corrupt and offensive to the scent, which must needs be very dangerous; for though the corruption of it cannot strike the outward parts of a man, yet by receiving it into our breathing organs (the nose or mouth), it is mortall and deadlie.

The Serpent or Dragon, as some call it, is reputed to be nine feet, or rather more, in length, and shaped almost in the form of the axle-tree of a cart; a quantitie of Thickness in the middest, and somewhat smaller at both ends.

The scales along his backe seem to be blackish, and so much as is discovered under his bellie, appeareth to be red; for I speak of no nearer description than a reasonable ocular distance; for coming too near it hath already been too dearlie pay'd for.

It is likewise discovered to have large feet, and rids away as fast as a man can run.

He is of countenance very proud, and at the sight or hearing of man or cattell, will raise his necke upright, and seem to listen and loke about with great arrogance.

There are likewise on either side of him discovered two great bunches, so big as a large foote ball, and as some think, will growe into wings. But God I hope will so defend the poore people of the neighbourhood, that he shall be destroyed before he growe so fledge.'

(*from an old printed document in the British Museum*)

# *from* Beowulf: Dragon Slayer

In the darkest hour of the spring night Grendel came to Heorot as he had come so many times before, up from his lair and over the high moors, through the mists that seemed to travel with him under the pale moon; Grendel, the Night-Stalker, the Death-Shadow. He came to the foreporch and snuffed about it, and smelled the man-smell, and found that the door which had stood unlatched for him so long was barred and bolted. Snarling in rage that any man should dare attempt to keep him out, he set the flat of his talon-tipped hands against the timbers and burst them in.

Dark as it was, the hall seemed to fill with a monstrous shadow at his coming; a shadow in which Beowulf, half springing up, then holding himself in frozen stillness, could make out no shape nor clear outline save two eyes filled with a wavering greenish flame.

The ghastly corpse-light of his own eyes showed Grendel the shapes of men as it seemed sleeping, and he did not notice among them one who leaned up on his elbow. Laughing in his throat, he reached out and grabbed young Hondscio who lay nearest to him, and almost before his victim had time to cry out, tore him limb from limb and drank the warm blood. Then, while the young warrior's dying shriek still hung upon the air, he reached for another. But this time his hand was met and seized in a grasp such as he had never felt before; a grasp that had in it the strength of thirty men. And for the first time he who had brought fear to so many caught the taste of it himself, knowing that at last he had met his match and maybe his master.

Beowulf leapt from the sleeping bench and grappled him in the darkness; and terror broke over Grendel in full force, the terror of a wild animal trapped; so that he thought no more of his hunting but only of breaking the terrible hold upon his arm and flying back into the night and the wilderness, and he howled and bellowed as he struggled for his freedom. Beowulf set his teeth and summoned all his strength and tightened his grip until the sinews cracked; and locked together they reeled and staggered up and down the great hall.

Trestles and sleeping benches went over with crash on crash as they strained this way and that, trampling even through the last red embers of the dying fire; and the very walls seemed to groan and shudder as though the stout timbers would burst apart. And all the while Grendel snarled and shrieked and Beowulf fought in silence save for his gasping breaths.

Outside, the Danes listened in horror to the turmoil that seemed as though it must split Heorot asunder; and within, the Geats had sprung from their sleeping benches sword in hand, forgetful of their powerlessness against the Troll-kind, but in the dark, lit only by stray gleams of bale-fire from the monster's eyes, they dared not strike for fear of slaying their leader, and when one or other of them did contrive to get in a blow, the sword blade glanced off Grendel's charmed hide as though he were sheathed in dragon scales.

At last, when the hall was wrecked to the walls, the Night-Stalker gathered himself for one last despairing effort to break free. Beowulf's hold was as fierce as ever; yet none the less the two figures burst apart – and Grendel with a frightful shriek staggered to the doorway and through it, and fled wailing into the night, leaving his arm and shoulder torn from the roots in the hero's still unbroken grasp.

*Rosemary Sutcliff*

## *The Boodlespook*

It's the boodlespook you nincompoop
Of course it's not a dwarf
He's really more than two foot four
But you see he has a stoop
And so would you with three left feet
Two size ten and one size eight
And a pair of arms too short to meet
It's the boodlespook you creep.
It's the boodlespook you utter clot
How can you say you think it's not
What else do you know that's only got
Eleven teeth, with nine on top
And two beneath, but the boodlespook?
It's the boodlespook you barnacle
Of course he wears a monocle
And so would you with just one eye
And that one pointing at the sky
It's the boodlespook you silly chump
It's nothing like a heffalump.
Does a heffalump have turquoise toes
Or a daffodil where its nose should grow
And do heffalumps talk spookabuzz?
Of course they don't, but the boodle does.
It's the boodlespook you drippy wet
I've told you now so don't forget
And if you see him walking by
Don't point or stare or give a cry
Or laugh at him – he's not a fluke
Remember now, he's the boodlespook.

## *A Short Litany*

From witches and wizards and longtail'd buzzards,
And creeping things that run in hedge bottoms,
Good Lord deliver us.

## *from* Macbeth

*First Witch:* Round about the cauldron go;
In the poison'd entrails throw.
Toad, that under cold stone
Days and nights hast thirty-one
Swelter'd venom sleeping got,
Boil thou first i' the charmed pot.

*All:* Double, double toil and trouble;
Fire burn and cauldron bubble.

*Second Witch:* Fillet of a fenny snake,
In the cauldron boil and bake;
Eye of newt, and toe of frog,
Wool of bat, and tongue of dog,
Adder's fork, and blind-worm's sting,
Lizard's leg, and howlet's wing,
For a charm of powerful trouble,
Like a hell-broth boil and bubble.

*All:* Double, double toil and trouble;
Fire burn and cauldron bubble.

*Third Witch:* Scale of dragon, tooth of wolf,
Witches' mummy, maw and gulf
Of the ravin'd salt-sea shark,
Root of hemlock digg'd i' the dark,
Liver of blaspheming Jew,
Gall of goat, and slips of yew
Silver's in the moon's eclipse,
Nose of Turk, and Tartar's lips,
Finger of birth-strangled babe
Ditch-deliver'd by a drab,
Make the gruel thick and slab:
Add thereto a tiger's chaudron
For the ingredients of our cauldron.

*All:* Double, double toil and trouble;
Fire burn and cauldron bubble.

## *A Charm against Witches*

Black-luggie, hammer-head,
Rowan-tree, and red thread
Put the warlocks to their speed.

# TONGUE TWISTER

Which is the witch that wished the wicked wish?

## Flower-charm ... to Enable one to See Fairies

Take a pint of sallet oyle and put in a vial glasse; and first wash it with rose-water; the flowers to be gathered towards the east. Wash it till the oyle becomes white, then put into the glasse, and then put thereto the buds of hollyhocke, the flowers of marygolde, the flowers or toppes of wild thyme, the budds of young hazle, and the thyme must be gathered near the side of a hill where fairies are use to be; and take the grasse of a fairy throne; then all these put into the glasse and set it to dissolve three days in the sunne and keep it for thy use.

(*from the Ashmolean Museum*, *Oxford*)

There was a young maid who said, 'Why
Can't I look in my ear with my eye?
If I give my mind to it,
I'm sure I can do it.
You never can tell till you try.'

I wish that my room had a floor
I don't care so much for a door;
But this walking around
Without touching the ground
Is getting to be quite a bore.

There are men in the village of Erith
Whom nobody seeth or heareth.
They spend hours afloat
In a flat-bottomed boat
Which nobody roweth or steereth.

## FAMOUS FALLACY

Did you know that:

The number thirteen *isn't* always considered an unlucky number? It was once thought to be a holy number which could bring great good fortune. It is still thought to be lucky to put a hen on a clutch of thirteen eggs.

# FASCINATING FACT

Did you know that:

A psychical researcher claimed recently that Britain has more ghosts per square mile than any other country in the world?

# RIDICULOUS RIDDLES

Q. What walks backwards through walls going 'Er, boo!'?

A. A nervous ghost.

Q. What is big and red and eats rocks?

A. A big red rock-eater.

Q. What's purple and has sixty legs and big teeth?

A. I've no idea, but if you meet one – *run*.

## *Playground Ghost Story*

There was a woman all skin and bone
Who lived in a cottage all on her own,
Oo-oo-oo!

She thought she'd go to church one day
To hear the parson preach and pray,
Oo-oo-oo!

When she got to the wooden stile
She thought she'd stay and rest a while,
Oo-oo-oo!

When she reached the old church door
A ghastly ghost lay on the floor,
Oo-oo-oo!

The grubs crawled in, the grubs crawled out,
Of its ears, eyes, nose and mouth.
Oo-oo-oo!

Oh, you ghastly ghost – she said –
Shall I be like you when I'm dead?
**Ye-ee-es!**

## Magic Boxes

Look hard at each of these boxes, one after the other, concentrating on each for a few minutes.

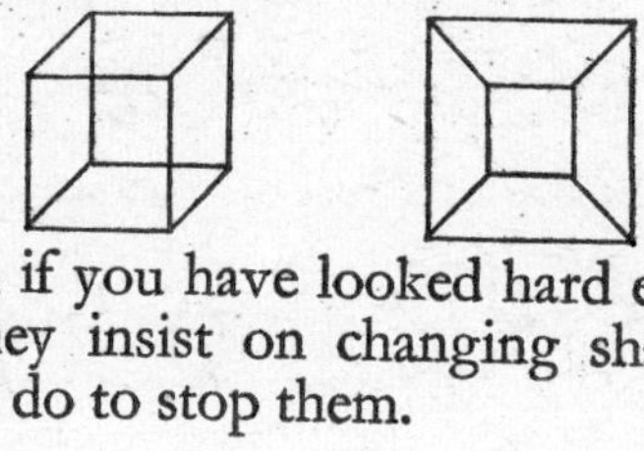

You will notice, if you have looked hard enough and long enough, that they insist on changing shape, and there's nothing you can do to stop them.

# MAKE YOUR OWN MAGIC

## The Mind-reading Trick

*You will need*
several pieces of paper
a pencil

Now, ask your audience to call out names of towns, or well-known personalities, and you write what you hear on the pieces of paper. These are then very carefully shuffled together in a hat, or bowl, and someone from the audience is asked to pick out one of the pieces, while all the rest are very carefully destroyed. After you have concentrated very hard for a moment or two you will be able to announce which name is written on the paper.

**How it is done**
It really couldn't be easier. When the names are being called out you write the *first* name given on *each* piece of paper, though it will look as if you are writing them all. The audience never sees the papers since you shuffle them with the blank sides upwards, and then destroy all but one. If you ask the person who picks the name out of the hat to look at it straight away and to concentrate on it very hard, while all the rest of the audience keeps very still and quiet so as not to distract either of you, they will be quite convinced that you are a mind-reader.

# The Mysterious Flame Trick

*You will need*
1 coloured candle
1 white candle
1 blindfold
1 box of matches

First of all, hand both the candles to your audience and ask them to look at them very carefully to see for themselves that they are perfectly ordinary. Next, ask that you should be blind-folded and given a volunteer to help with the trick. Turn your back while he chooses one of the candles and lights it. After a moment's concentration you will be able to tell the audience which of the candles is burning.

**How it is done**
Again, it's very simple. When you take back the candles after the audience has examined them you secretly wet the wick of one of them with saliva. If the volunteer chooses that one it will make a tiny spluttering noise when it is lit. If he chooses the other, the only sound will be that of the match. Make the trick as dramatic as possible to persuade the audience that it is much more complicated than it really is.

# The Disappearing Coin Trick

*You will need*
1 handkerchief
1 coin
1 piece of plasticine

To start with, spread a clean handkerchief on the table and ask one of the audience to put a small coin in the middle of it. You will then be able to fold up the handkerchief, utter a magic spell, and open it out again to show your astonished friends that the coin has vanished.

**How it is done**
This one is just a little more difficult, but very effective. Before the trick begins you should have fixed a small knob of plasticine to one corner of the handkerchief. While you have it spread out on the table you must keep the plasticine covered with your finger tips. When one of your friends has put a coin in place, fold over the corner so that the plasticine covers the coin. Then fold in the other corners on top of the first, and press down hard while you chant your favourite magic spell. Now, pick up the handkerchief by the two new corners you have made nearest to you, and show it to your audience. The coin will have vanished from the centre, and will be fastened inside the corner hanging down so that no-one can see it. Finally, take the corner with the coin attached in your right hand and hold on to the coin while you pull the handkerchief up with your left hand, shake it out, and hand it round for the audience to examine.

And finally, to finish with a flourish –

# The Miraculous Wineglass

*You will need*
1 wineglass
dress-making pins
water

**How it is done**
Fill the glass with water to the brim. Ask your audience to guess how many pins can be dropped into the water before the already-full glass overflows. Now drop the pins in, very gently, one by one, points downwards. Everyone will be amazed to discover that you can put in at least two hundred pins, and instead of spilling over, the water will seem to rise above the level of the top of the glass. There's no trickery about this one – it just happens.

# *from* Revelations

After this I looked, and, behold, a door was opened in heaven: and the first voice which I heard was as it were of a trumpet talking with me; which said, Come up hither, and I will shew thee things which must be hereafter.
And immediately I was in the spirit: and, behold, a throne was set in heaven, and one sat on the throne.
And he that sat was to look upon like a jasper and a sardine stone: and there was a rainbow round about the throne, in sight like unto an emerald.
And round about the throne were four and twenty seats: and upon the seats I saw four and twenty elders sitting, clothed in white raiment; and they had on their heads crowns of gold.
And out of the throne proceeded lightnings and thunderings and voices: and there were seven lamps of fire burning before the throne, which are the seven Spirits of God.
And before the throne there was a sea of glass like unto crystal: and in the midst of the throne, and round about the throne, were four beasts full of eyes before and behind.
And the first beast was like a lion, and the second beast like a calf, and the third beast had a face as a man, and the fourth beast was like a flying eagle.
And the four beasts had each of them six wings about him; and they were full of eyes within: and they rest not day and night, saying, Holy, holy, holy, Lord God Almighty, which was, and is, and is to come.

## *from* Under Milk Wood

There's the clip clop of horses on the sunhoneyed cobbles of the humming streets, hammering of horse-shoes, gobble quack and cackle, tomtit twitter from the bird-ounced boughs, braying on Donkey Down. Bread is baking, pigs are grunting, chop goes the butcher, milk-churns bell, tills ring, sheep cough, dogs shout, saws sing. Oh, the Spring whinny and morning moo from the clog dancing farms, the gulls' gab and rabble on the boat-bobbing river and sea and the cockles bubbling in the sand, scamper of sanderlings, curlew cry, crow caw, pigeon coo, clock strike, bull bellow, and the ragged gabble of the beargarden school as the women scratch and babble in Mrs Organ Morgan's general shop where everything is sold: custard, buckets, henna, rat-traps, shrimp-nets, sugar, stamps, confetti, paraffin, hatchets, whistles.

*Dylan Thomas*

Can you give a complete English sentence in which the word 'and' appears five times in succession? What about this one? 'When I looked at the sign hanging outside the inn, I noticed that the spaces between "Pig" and "And" and "And" and "Whistle" were of different sizes.'

## *Punctuation Puzzle*

Caesar entered on his head
A helmet on each foot
A sandal in his hand he had
His trusty sword to boot.

# BRAIN BOTHER

If Sloane Square = Slogger Squagger
And if Golders Green = Goggers Gregger
– What is a waste paper basket?

A wagger pagger bagger

## *Speech Day*

Ladles and Jellyspoons,
I stand upon this speech to make a platform,
The train I arrived in has not yet come,
So I took a bus and walked.
I come before you
To stand behind you
And tell you something
I know nothing about.

# *The Computer's First Christmas Card*

jollymerry
hollyberry
jollyberry
merryholly
happyjolly
jollyjelly
jellybelly
bellymerry
hollyheppy
jollyMolly
marryJerry
merryHarry
hoppyBarry
heppyJarry
boppyheppy
berryjorry
jorryjolly
moppyjelly
Mollymerry
Jerryjolly
bellyboppy
jorryhoppy
hollymoppy
Barrymerry
Jarryhappy
happyboppy
boppyjolly
jollymerry
merrymerry
merrymerry
merryChris
ammerryasa
Chrismerry
as MERRYCHR
YSANTHEMUM

*Edwin Morgan*

## *from* The Wonderful O

That night in the tavern, after his thirteenth pint of rum, Black began to sing a ditty in a voice that had the timbre of a buzzard's:

'I won't go down the horrible street
To see the horrible people.
I'll gladly climb the terrible stair
That leads to the terrible steeple
And the terrible bats, and the terrible rats,
And the cats in the terrible steeple.
But I won't go down the horrible street
To see the horrible people.'

As he sang, the taverners stared at him and then they left their drinks unfinished, paid for them, and slunk away into the night.

'Methinks the people have a loathing for your voice and for your song,' said Littlejack.

'I'll take away from them,' said Black, 'everything that plays and has an O.'

And so the following morning the crew went from house to house, seizing violins and cellos, trombones, horns, and oboes, pianos, harpsichords and clavicords, accordions and melodeons, bassoons and saxaphones, and all the other instruments with O's, up to and including the woodwinds. A man and his wife who loved to play duets on mandolin and glockenspiel drifted apart. Children, forbidden the use of combs, could no longer play tunes on combs with tissue paper. The crew spent the afternoon breaking up an old calliope they had found rusting in a field, and taking apart a carillon.

'All they have is fifes and drums and cymbals,' gloated Black.

'And zithers and guitars,' said Littlejack. 'And dulcimers and spinets, and bugles, harps, and trumpets.'

'Much good they'll get from these,' said Black, 'or any others. I haven't finished with the O's in music, in harmony and melody, that is, and compositions. They'll have no score, and what is more, no orchestra, or podium, or baton, and no conductor. They can't play symphonies, or rhapsodies, sonatas or concerti. I'll take away their oratorios and choirs and choruses, and all their soloists, their baritones and tenors and sopranos, their altos and contraltos and accompanists. All they'll have is the funeral march, the chant and anthem, and the dirge, and certain snatches.'

'They'll still have serenades,' said Littlejack.

Black made an evil and impatient gesture. 'You can't serenade a lady on a balcony,' he said, 'if there isn't any balcony. Let them hum their hymns and lisp their litanies.' Black's eyes began to glow as he named O-names that would have to go: 'Scherzo, largo, and crescendo, allegro and diminuendo. Let the lyric writers have their Night in June. Much good it'll do 'em without the moon.'

*James Thurber*

# *The Kangaroo's Coff*

A Poem for Children Ill in Bed, Indicating to Them the Oddities of our English Orthography.

The eminent Professor Hoff
Kept, as a pet, a Kangaroo
Who, one March day, started a coff
That very soon turned into floo.

Before the flu carried him off
To hospital (still with his coff),
A messenger came panting through
The door, and saw the Kangarough.

The Kangaroo lay wanly there
Within the Prof's best big armchere,
Taking (without the power to chew)
A sip of lemonade or tew.

'O Kangaroo,' the fellow said,
'I'm glad you're not already daid,
For I have here (pray do not scoff)
Some stuff for your infernal coff.

'If you will take these powdered fleas,
And just a tiny lemon squeas
Mixed with a little plain tapwater,
They'll cure you. Or at least they ater.'

Prof Hoff then fixed the medicine,
Putting the fleas and lemon ine
A glass of water, which he brought
The Kangaroo as he'd been tought.

The Kangaroo drank down the draught,
Shivered and scowled – then oddly laught
And vaulted out of the armchair
Before the Prof's astonished stair –

Out of the window, in the air,
Up to the highest treetop whair
He sat upon the topmost bough
And chortled down, 'Look at me nough!'

The messenger would not receive
Reward for this, but answered, 'Weive
Done our best, and that's reward
Enough, my very learned lard'

(By which he meant Professor Hoff).
As for the Kangaroo, he blew
A kiss down as the man rode off,
A cured and happy Kangarew –

As you may be, when you have read
This tale I wrote lying in bead.

*Anthony Thwaite*

## A Few Twisters to Tangle your Tongue

A noisy noise annoys an oyster.

Naughty Nettie's knitting knotted nighties for the Navy.

Double bubble gum bubbles double.

We surely shall see the sun shine soon.

Charles Cholmondley-Churchill cheerfully chases Chichester's chess champion.

He ran from the Indies to the Andes in his undies.

I never felt felt that felt like that felt felt.

## Now Twist your own Twister

Begin by writing a sentence in which all the words begin with the same sound, like 'Mighty Micky Mouse makes mischief'. Experiment until you find some that twist your tongue into knots.

Then you can be more ambitious and make twisters that use two different sounds, like 'The sixth sheik's sick sheep's sicker'. Notice how confused the 's' and 'sh' sounds become when you say that quickly.

One of the shortest tongue-twisters is supposed to be the hardest in our language. It is:

PEGGY BABCOCK

See how often you can say it before it defeats you.

# Pun Page

'Ring the bells,' said the vicar, appealingly.

'Come in and see my new three-piece,' she said suitely.

'I have mown the lawn,' he said, lackadaisically.

'Two chops, please,' they said, jointly.

'Just look at those rafters,' she beamed.

**In the Library**

*The Cliff Accident*, by Eileen Dover
*Will She Come*, by Sheila Rive
*Emergency Ward*, by Ida Payne
*The Plump One*, by Henrietta Lotte
*Loud Rumblings*, by M. T. Tumm

**In the Art Gallery**

*Jungle Giants*, by L. E. Fant
*Breakfast Table*, by M. N. Eggs
*Signpost*, by Hugo Yorway
*A Funeral*, by Diane B. Buried
*Back from Holiday*, by Geoff A. Nicetime

# Pick yourself a Palindrome

Palindromes have always been popular.
Adam used one when he introduced himself to Eve. He said,
'Madam, I'm Adam.'
Napoleon had a go too, when he announced,
'Able, was I, ere I saw Elba.'
And the composer, Henry Purcell, is supposed to have declared,
'Egad, a base tone denotes a bad age.'

Here are a few more.
'Rats live on no evil star.'
'Rise to vote, sir.'
'Not on!'
'Now stop, Major General, are negro jam pots won?'

What is a palindrome? Read all these sentences backwards, and you'll find out. Perhaps you can make up one of your own?

## *Silly Story*

'Twas in the month of Liverpool
In the city of July,
The snow was raining heavily,
The streets were very dry.
The flowers were sweetly singing,
The birds were in full bloom,
When I went to the cellar
To look for an upstairs room.
I saw two thousand miles away
A house just out of sight,
It stood between two others,
Its walls were black-washed white.

# Riddles

Two legs sat upon three legs
With one leg in his lap;
In comes four legs,
Runs away with one leg,
Up jumps two legs,
Picks up three legs,
Throws it after four legs,
And makes him bring back one leg.

Laura has a large one in front. Paul has a little one behind. And poor Miss Milligan had two in the middle until she married Mr Brown.

Q. What is it?

A. The letter 'l'.

Little Nancy Netticoat
Wears a white petticoat,
The longer she lives
The shorter she grows,
Little Nancy Netticoat.

Q. What is she?

A. A lighted candle

# A Cockney Alphabet

A horses
B mutton
C the Highlanders
D dumb
E brick
F vescence
G police
H it
I looting
J oranges
K a cuppa
L leather
M sis
N eggs
O my dead body
P a penny
Q the flicks
R mo
S you
T two
U mism
V la France
W a pound
X breakfast
Y girl-friend
Z his hat

# A Cockney Alphabet Explained

A 'Ay for 'Orses
B Beef or mutton
C Seaforth Highlanders
D Deef or dumb
E 'Eave a brick
F Effervescence
G Chief of Police
H 'Ate ye for it
I 'Igh falutin'
J Jaffa oranges
K Cafe for a cuppa
L 'Ell for leather
M Emphasis
N 'En for eggs
O Over my dead body
P Pee for a penny
Q Queue for the flicks
R 'Alf a mo'
S As for you . . .
T Tea for two
U Euphemism
V Vive la France
W Double you for a pound
X Eggs for breakfast
Y Wife or girl-friend?
Z 'S head for 'is 'at.

## *Country Counting – One to Twenty*

Yahn, Tayn, Tether, Mether, Mumph,
Hither, Lither, Auver, Dauver, Dic,
Yahndic, Tayndic, Tetherdic, Metherdic, Mumphit,
Yahn a mumphit, Tayn a mumphit,
Tethera mumphit, Methera mumphit, Jig it.

# FASCINATING FACTS

Did you know that:

Both 'facetious' and 'abstemious' contain all five vowels, once only, and in the right order?

'Uncomplimentary' contains all five vowels, once only, and in reverse order?

The shortest place-names in the world are Y (France), A (Norway), U (Caroline Islands), and O (Japan)?

The longest place-name in the world is – 'TAUMATAWHAKATANGIHANGAKOAUAUOTAMATEA (TURIPUKAKAPIKIMAUNGAHORONUKU) POKAIWHENUAKITANATAHU'. It means 'the place where Tamatea, the man with the big knee who slid, climbed and swallowed mountains, known as Land-eater, played on his flute to his loved one.' It is the Maori name for a hill in North Island, New Zealand.

There once was a very old gnu,
Who was used by a chef in some stew.
He should have been told
The gnu was too old:
For stews, only new gnus will do.

She frowned and called him Mr.
Because he boldly kr.
And so in spite
That very night
This Mr. kr. sr.

A flea and a fly in a flue
Were imprisoned, so what could they do?
Said the fly, 'Let us flee,'
Said the flea, 'Let us fly,'
So they flew through a flaw in the flue.

## *This is the End*

He rocked the boat,
Did Ezra Shank.
These bubbles o
o
o
o mark
Where Ezra sank.

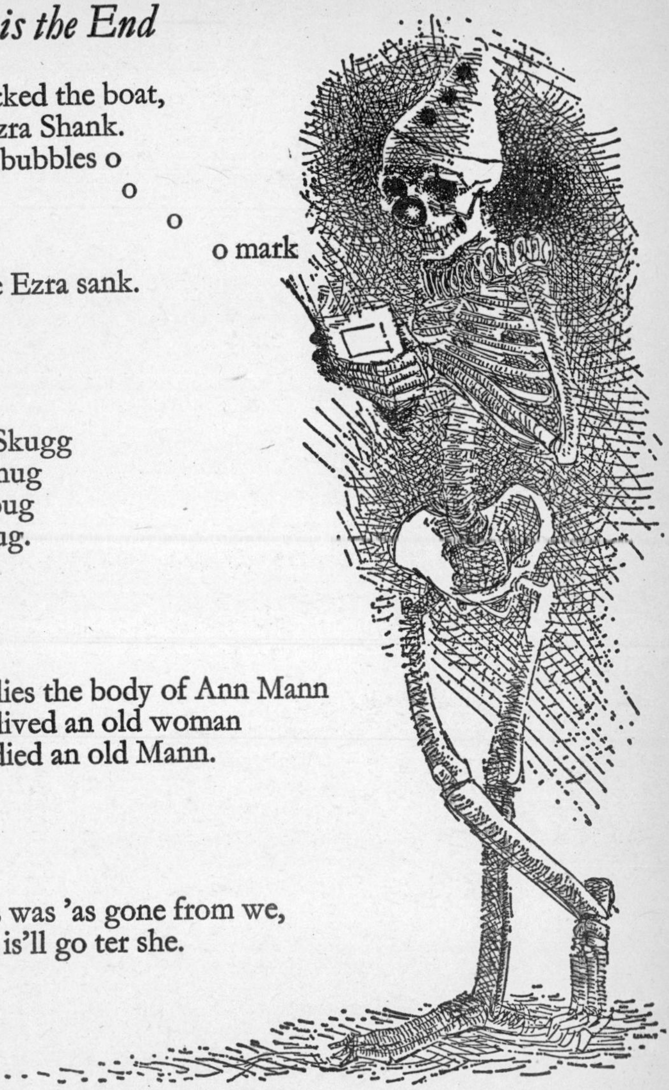

Here Skugg
Lies snug
As a bug
In a rug.

Here lies the body of Ann Mann
Who lived an old woman
And died an old Mann.

'Er as was 'as gone from we,
Us as is'll go ter she.

Here lies what's left of William Dough –
With us he is no more,
For what he thought was $H_2O$
Was $H_2SO_4$

# *A Lyke-wake Dirge*

This ae night, this ae night,
Every night and all,
Fire, and fleet, and candle-light,
And Christ receive thy soul.

When thou from hence away art passed,
Every night and all,
To Whinny-muir thou comest at last,
And Christ receive thy soul.

If ever thou gavest hosen and shoon,
Every night and all,
Sit thee down and put them on,
And Christ receive thy soul.

If hosen and shoon thou ne'er gavest nane,
Every night and all,
The whinnies shall prick thee to the bare bane,
And Christ receive thy soul.

From Whinny-muir when thou mayest pass,
Every night and all,
To Brig o' Dread thou comest at last
And Christ receive thy soul.

From Brig o' Dread when thou mayest pass,
Every night and all,
To purgatory fire thou comest at last
And Christ receive thy soul.

If ever thou gavest meat or drink,
Every night and all,
The fire shall never make thee shrink
And Christ receive thy soul.

If meat or drink thou ne'er gavest nane,
Every night and all,
The fire will burn thee to the bare bane,
And Christ receive thy soul.

This ae night, this ae night,
Every night and all,
Fire, and fleet, and candle-light,
And Christ receive thy soul.

## Solution to the Matchstick Fish Brain-botherer

Remove matchsticks numbers 1, 5 and 8 and replace as shown here, in black.

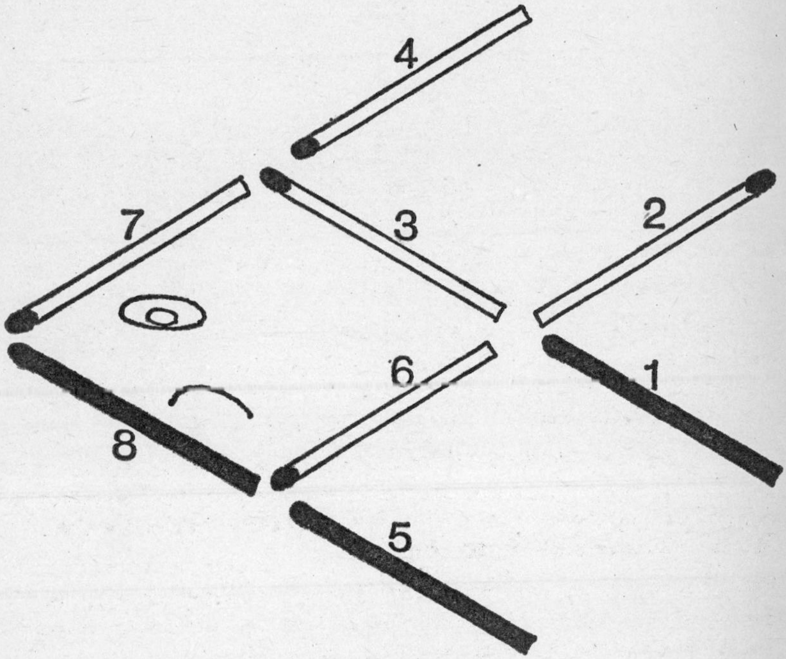

# More Beaver Books

We hope you have enjoyed this Beaver Book. Here are some of the other titles:

**Animal Quiz** Johnny Morris, universally known and loved for his television programme Animal Magic, has created a picture quiz book about all sorts of animals, fish and birds, full of fun and fact for all the family

**White Fang** Jack London's great classic story about the life of a wild wolf dog at the time of the Gold Rush in the Yukon

**Tales told near a Crocodile** Humphrey Harman has lived and worked for half a lifetime near Lake Victoria, the setting for these stories of African magic, legend and adventure. An evocative and fascinating collection of folk tales; with illustrations

**The Glass Knife** John Tully's gripping and intriguing story about a boy who has been reared to become a human sacrifice. Set in South America before the European discovery of the New World; illustrated by Victor Ambrus

**The Last of the Vikings** Henry Treece's exciting story, in the saga tradition, about the young Harald Hardrada, King of Norway; with superb illustrations by Charles Keeping

**Who Knows?** Twelve unsolved mysteries involving sudden death, mysterious disappearances and hidden treasure; by Jacynth Hope-Simpson

New Beavers are published every month and if you would like the *Beaver Bulletin* – which gives all the details – please send a large stamped addressed envelope to:

**Beaver Bulletin**
The Hamlyn Group
Astronaut House
Feltham
Middlesex TW14 9AR

371271